Assessment of Learning

Wynne Harlen

SAGE Publications
Los Angeles • London • New Delhi • Singapore

First published 2007

Sage Publications Ltd
A SAGE Publications Company
1 Oliver's Yard
London EC1Y 1SP

SAGE Publications Inc
2455 Teller Road
Thousand Oaks, California 91320

SAGE Publications India Pvt Ltd
B1/I1 Mohan Cooperative Industrial Area
Mathura Road, Post Bag 7
New Delhi 110 044

SAGE Publications Asia-Pacific Pte Ltd
33 Pekin Street #02-01
Far East Square
Singapore 048763

British Library Cataloguing in Publication data

A catalogue record for this book is available from the British Library

Library of Congress Control Number: 2006939847

ISBN 978-1-4129-3518-0
ISBN 978-1-4129-3519-7 (pbk)

Typeset by Dorwyn, Wells, Somerset
Printed in India at Replika Press Pvt. Ltd
Printed on paper from sustainable resources

Assessment of Learning

Contents

List of figures and tables

Acknowledgements

This book arose out of the work of a project, Assessment Systems for the Future (ASF), that had summative assessment as its focus. The project was set up by the Assessment Reform Group (ARG) and was funded by the Nuffield Foundation from 2003 to 2006. It worked through a series of meetings of an advisory group and seminars at which the advisory group members were joined by invited experts on various issues related to the role of teachers in the summative assessment of students' learning.

All the activities of the project and four working papers that captured the thinking and evidence at various stages can be found in the ASF pages of the ARG website. So this is not 'the book of the project' and does not attempt to describe the various transactions. In fact there are few direct references to the project events; the aim is to bring together, and in several parts to update and supplement, the arguments and research evidence used by the project in reaching its conclusions. The main ideas were ones that were developed collectively and my role as author has been to try to present them here as clearly and faithfully as possible. Nevertheless, I take responsibility for their final expression.

In Chapter 6 particularly I have drawn upon material that was written by members of the group and acknowledge the particular sources in footnotes. I am grateful to them and to all members of the group, listed below, who have freely given their time and shared their ideas throughout the project.

Members of the ASF project advisory group

David Bartlett
Paul Black
Richard Daugherty
Kathryn Ecclestone
Janet English
John Gardner

Carolyn Hutchinson
Mary James
Martin Montgomery
Paul Newton
Catrin Roberts
Jon Ryder
Judy Sebba
Gordon Stobart
Anne Whipp

Introduction

Background

Assessment of students' learning is an essential part of education, in which it takes several roles. The aim of this book is to consider how to conduct assessment for one of the main purposes – to summarize achievements in order to record and report on learning to those who need this information. As indicated in the acknowledgements, this book originates from work initiated by the Assessment Reform Group (ARG).

This voluntary group of researchers has, from its inception in 1989 as a policy task group of the British Educational Research Association, aimed to bring research evidence to bear on assessment policy and practice. Although always concerned with educational assessment for a range of purposes, the ARG is probably best known for bringing together research on the use of assessment to help learning, that is formative assessment or assessment for learning as it is also known. Thus the focus of this book – the assessment of learning or summative assessment – may need some explanation.

Rationale

The impact of 'high stakes' summative assessment

There are several reasons for concern about the impact of the process and uses of summative assessment that followed from changes in education policy made in the UK, as in many other countries, in the 1990s. The criticisms focus on the use of external tests, their impact being exacerbated through using test and examination results as the sole basis for target-setting and the evaluation of teachers, schools and education authorities. These concerns were not new. Already in the early 1990s there was a good deal of research evidence of the negative impact of frequent 'high stakes' testing on the curriculum and teaching from the earlier introduction of state-mandated testing in the USA (see for example Resnick and Resnick, 1992), and a growing realization about the low dependability of tests and examinations (Satterly, 1994). The ARG added to this evidence by reviewing research on the impact of testing on students' motivation for learning, finding strong evidence of negative impact (ARG, 2002a). This review also confirmed the impact on teachers and teaching, noting that

- When passing tests is high stakes (that is, the results are used for making decisions that affect the status or future of students, teachers or schools), teachers adopt a teaching style that emphasises transmission teaching of knowledge, thereby favouring those students who prefer to learn by mastering information presented sequentially. This disadvantages and lowers the self-esteem of those who prefer more active and creative learning experiences.
- External tests have a constricting effect on the curriculum, resulting in emphasis on subjects tested at the expense of creativity and personal and social development.
- High stakes tests often result in a great deal of time being spent on practice tests, with test performance being highly valued and other pupil achievements undervalued.
- Teachers can be very effective in training students to pass tests even when the students do not have the understanding or higher order thinking skills that the tests are intended to measure.
- Teachers' own assessments become mainly summative in function rather than formative.

Moreover it was clear that there was a mismatch between the widely recognised importance of preparing students for life in an increasingly changing and technological world and what was being taught, as dictated by tests. It is generally agreed that what is required is a curriculum designed to develop the ability to access and evaluate information, to apply knowledge to new situations and, importantly, to acquire the prerequisites for continued learning throughout life. Using tests as measures of the outcomes of education reflects and encourages a narrow and naïve view of learning, and the more serious the decisions resting on test scores (the higher the stakes) the greater the demand for 'accuracy', with the consequence that the tests are reduced to aspects of performance that can be unambiguously marked as correct or incorrect. When national policy encourages judgment of schools and teachers on the basis of the performance of their students on such tests, 'teaching to the test' becomes even more damaging to students' learning experience in school.

Impact on formative assessment

Given the ARG's conviction of the strength of evidence for using assessment for learning, it is not surprising that one of the key factors in directing attention to summative assessment was the impact of tests in inhibiting the development of formative assessment in practice. There was clearly a mismatch between the rhetoric of official documents and what happens in classrooms. Using assessment for learning has been included in the text of various new 'national strategies' introduced by the DfES (Department for Education and Skills) in England. While this is to be welcomed there is some evidence that the interpretation and implementation in practice tend to be mechanistic and lacking in signalling the essential shift in pedagogy that using assessment for learning requires. It is useful to recall that this is not the first time that formative assessment appears to have been welcomed and yet is still missing when ideas are translated into practice. Although the political context was notably different in 1989, the following example of the Task Group on Assessment and Testing (TGAT) serves both to illustrate the point and to explain how the system which is causing current concern originated.

When the TGAT reported on how to implement the student assessment introduced in the Education Reform Act of 1988, its recommendation that the assessment should serve a formative as well as a summative purpose was approved. However, the formative purpose was absent from the arrangements that were put in place; the main focus was on formal, time-limited, external tests whose results could be aggregated as indicators of the performance of teachers, schools, local education authorities and the system as a whole (Daugherty and Ecclestone, 2006). At the time the policy applied to England and Wales, and although Northern Ireland and Scotland had more leeway to create their own policies, there was an expectation that similar approaches would be introduced.

Since that time, the constitutional changes of 1999 have resulted in Scotland, Wales and Northern Ireland moving away from the use of tests and rejecting the evaluation of teachers and schools based solely on student performance results. The work of the ARG and indeed of the ASF project may well have been influential in these policy changes, as acknowledged by the Minister of Education in the Welsh Assembly Government (Davidson, 2006). Meanwhile, despite the embracing of assessment for learning in strategy documents, the policy in England remains one that creates a classroom and school ethos that research shows favours repeated summative assessment and inhibits the formative use of assessment (Pollard and Triggs, 2000).

The aims of this book

Of course summative assessment is an important and necessary part of education and of students' experience. In seeking to ensure that it can reflect the important outcomes of a modern education, that it is fair, dependable and has a positive role and value commensurate with its cost in terms of time and resources, we have looked for alternatives to depending on external testing and examinations. The use of teachers' judgments has many suitable properties, but it is not without problems. This book sets out to consider and to draw some conclusions from research and practice in seeking to weigh up the pros and cons of different approaches to summative assessment.

Inevitably, work conducted in the UK exists within the context of policies in the countries that make up the UK and in particular England, as the foreground. However, there is no doubt that the same issues arise in other countries where frequent student testing has been introduced, or is contemplated, often in the belief that testing raises standards. Whilst solutions have to be sought against a background of the social, historical and cultural context of a particular system, the discussion and examples in this book may be of use in clarifying options and foreseeing the possible consequences of policy decisions.

Structure and Content

The nine chapters of this short book fall into three main parts.

Part I – Assessment of Learning in Context

The first – assessment of learning in context – begins with the dull but necessary clarification of terms, since the words 'assessment' and 'evaluation' are often used with different meanings and sometimes interchangeably. The opening chapter then sets out a framework for describing the components of an assessment system, making clear that there are numerous ways in which the necessary components of an assessment system can be implemented. Each has to be 'fit for purpose' and one of the points emerging from the evidence in the book is that using assessment results for several purposes may well mean that they do not fit well all, or perhaps any, of these purposes. Also introduced are the four key properties that need to be optimised in making decisions about methods of student assessment. These are (construct) validity, reliability, positive impact on learning and effective use of resources; these are referred to on several occasions as the basis for evaluating assessment procedures.

The next two chapters in Part 1 are essentially concerned with validity, that is, with the question of what we should be including in summative assessment. Chapter 2 makes reference to statements from organizations such as the OECD (the Organisation for Economic Co-operation and Development), from government departments and from researchers about the importance of designing the curriculum to enable students to learn with understanding, to understand how to learn, to develop scientific and technological literacy, citizenship, creativity and economic productivity. However, unless these outcomes are included in what is assessed, they may not be taken seriously. The possibilities of assessing such outcomes are discussed, making a case for moving beyond testing. Chapter 3 gives some evidence about the information that is needed from summative assessment by some of the 'users' of results – the teachers, the students themselves, parents, employers, trainers and higher and further education admission tutors.

In the light of what emerges as to the kinds of information that ought to be included in valid summative assessment, the fourth chapter returns to the four properties of assessment introduced in Chapter 1 and uses them as criteria for evaluating different ways of assessment intended learning. Assessment procedures for three particular uses are considered – to help learning, to summarize learning for internal school purposes and to summarize for external uses. The discussion leads to a 'balance-sheet' of pros and cons in relation to conducting summative assessment by tests or by using teachers' judgments. This sets the scene for Part 2 which examines the use of teachers' judgments for assessment of learning in practice.

Part 2 – Using Teachers' Judgments for Assessment of Learning in Practice

Part 2, then, begins by addressing one of the main potential weaknesses of using teachers' judgments: their low reliability. Evidence from a systematic review of research on the validity and reliability of summative assessment carried out by teachers is used to identify the conditions that favour greater reliability in using teachers' judgments. These conditions include the existence and use of criteria that indicate progression in learning, in terms that help to identify relevant evidence but do not limit the range of learning experiences, and attention to quality enhancement. The last section of the chapter outlines some advantages and disadvantages of various approaches to quality assurance and quality control, drawing on earlier ARG work (Harlen, 1994).

Chapters 6 and 7 comprise critical accounts of existing procedures that include the use of assessment by teachers or trainers. Chapter 6 takes these examples from England: the Foundation Stage Profile introduced in 2003, the teacher assessed element of the end of Key Stage assessment, and the National Vocational Qualifications. The degree to which criteria are spelled out in detail varies considerably in these examples, highlighting the difficulty in finding the optimum level of detail that supports reliable assessment by teachers. This theme also emerges in Chapter 7, which considers examples from outside England: from Scotland, Wales and Northern Ireland, from Australia and from the USA. Other themes identified as affecting the success of procedures using teachers' assessment include the key role of moderation, particularly in the form of group discussion of students' work, the disassociation of individual student data from school accountability procedures, and the relationship between formative and summative purposes of assessment.

Part 3 – Changing Practice and Policy

Part 3, 'Changing Practice and Policy', comprises the final two chapters of the book which take up the two most fundamental issues that have permeated all other chapters and have just been mentioned as prominent in Chapter 7. First is the relationship between formative and summative assessment. As noted earlier, a prime reason for embarking on this study was the evidence of the tendency for tests used summative assessment, especially when high stakes are attached to the results, to dominate the assessment culture of a classroom and to deter the use of assessment to help learning. The arguments subsequently put forward in Chapter 8 lead on to the position that summative assessment can be conducted in ways that encourage formative assessment. Nevertheless the two purposes that they serve are essentially separate and the difference in how they are conducted cannot be ignored. These emerge from a discussion of the characteristics of assessment for each purpose. In particular the criteria used in making judgments vary in detail and origin, thus making it essential to distinguish between evidence and the interpretation of evidence. Taking these differences into account, a model is proposed of a process in which evidence collected by teachers and students as part of regular work is gradually accumulated and reinterpreted against criteria, at those times when it is necessary to report on learning. The model gives a role in summative assessment to students, of the kind which they do not have in external tests, and makes the process of judgment a more open one.

Finally, Chapter 9 widens the discussion to include those parts of an assessment system that deal with accountability and system monitoring. The four criteria relating to the desirable properties of assessment are applied to different procedures for serving these two purposes. This leads to the conclusion that the information used in evaluating schools and holding them accountable should include far more than student assessment data. In the case of system monitoring there is clear evidence that using results from national tests does not provide a valid or reliable basis for deciding whether standards of achievement are changing. What is needed is a programme of regular surveys that enable subject domains to be properly assessed and which involve only a sample of students at any one time.

Chapter 9 also brings together various threads in earlier discussions that point to what may need to be changed if summative assessment is to be improved. These include expressing the curriculum so that it genuinely reflects the outcomes that Chapter 2 showed to be necessary, and assessment criteria that clarify progression and indicate key aspects of classroom work that are evidence of achievement. Another point addressed here is the role that special tasks or tests can take in a summative assessment system that is essentially teacher-based. Also discussed is the need for transparency in assessment procedures and some rethinking of how teachers spend their time as assessment becomes a more central part of their professional work. These and other points are combined in the implications for policy-makers and practitioners that conclude the book.

PART 1 Assessment of Learning in Context

1 Meanings, processes and properties of assessment

This chapter lays the ground for later chapters by setting out the meaning of terms that are used to describe, analyse and evaluate assessment procedures and systems. In particular it makes clear that the word 'assessment' is used to refer to the process of gathering, interpreting and using evidence to make judgments about students' achievements in education. The term 'evaluation' is reserved for this process of using evidence in relation to programmes, procedures, materials or systems. It also makes explicit the meaning of 'assessment by teachers' or 'teachers' assessment', terms that will feature frequently throughout this book.

A framework of variables within seven main components of assessment is offered as a way of describing different ways of conducting assessment. Finally, properties that need to be considered in making decisions about how to conduct summative assessment are proposed: validity, reliability, impact and use of resources.

Introduction

Any discussion of assessment inevitably involves reference to concepts that are special to the subject – jargon to those not familiar with the terms. Whilst trying to avoid this as far as possible, it is important to use words with some precision in developing arguments relating to topics as complex as assessment. So, although it makes a rather dry start to the book, the matter of terminology used in discussing assessment cannot be avoided. Words such as assessment, evaluation, testing, performance, achievement, formative, summative and so on will have to be used in this book and, without intending to suggest what is correct or incorrect usage, it is essential that their meaning as used here is clear and consistent. It is best to get this done sooner rather than later and to be candid about how difficult it is to be precise.

As part of this clarification, the second section of this introductory chapter looks at how types of assessment can be described in terms of the various ways in which it can be carried out. In the third section, we consider some key properties that ought to be taken into account when evaluating the effectiveness and value of any type of assessment. These properties are revisited throughout the book, in the course of providing evidence and arguments for proposing reform in assessment systems that rely heavily on external tests and examinations.

Meanings

Assessment and Evaluation

Assessment and evaluation both describe a process of collecting and interpreting evidence for some purpose. They both involve decisions about what evidence to use, the collection of that evidence in a systematic and planned way, the interpretation of the evidence to produce a judgment, and the communication and use of that judgment. The evidence, of whatever kind, is only ever an indication or sample of a wider range that could be used.

The terms 'evaluation' and 'assessment' in education are sometimes used with different meanings, but also interchangeably. In some countries, including the USA, the term 'evaluation' is often used to refer to individual student achievement, which in other countries including the UK is described as 'assessment'. In the UK 'evaluation' is more often used to denote the process of collecting evidence and making judgments about programmes, systems, materials, procedures and processes; 'assessment' refers to the process of collecting evidence and making judgments relating to outcomes, such as students' achievement of particular goals of learning or teachers' and others' understanding. The processes of assessment and evaluation are similar but the kinds of evidence, the purpose and the basis on which judgments are made, differ. Our concern here is assessment in this latter sense; that is, the evidence is about what students can do, what they know or how they behave and the judgments are about their achievements.

Assessment Systems

'System' implies a whole comprised of parts that are connected to each other. In the case of assessment the system will include: procedures for collecting evidence, its use for different purposes, and how it will be used for individual reporting, certification and selection; system monitoring at local and national levels; the use of measures of performance of students in the accountability of teachers and schools; the role of teachers in assessment, both formative and summative; the moderation of teachers' judgments;

and the way in which evidence from different sources, such as assessment by teachers and external tests, is combined.

We need look no further than either side of the border between Scotland and England to appreciate the difference between assessment systems. In Scotland summative assessment of pupils up to the age of 15 or 16 is for internal school use only. There is a nation-wide programme for implementing formative assessment. Achievement is reported to students and parents about twice a year in terms of levels, but there is no central collection of these results and they are not used for national monitoring or for creating league tables of schools (although school results are published for the external testing at age 15–16). Individual student assessment is based on teachers' judgments, moderated by the use of external tests administered by teachers when they judge students as able to pass a test at a certain level. National monitoring is conducted through a separate programme of testing which involves samples of pupils at certain ages.

By contrast, in England a combination of national testing and teachers' judgments is used for internal summative assessment and national test results are used for monitoring performance of students at age 7, 11 and 14 year on year. National test results are also to evaluate the performance of schools, local authorities and the country as a whole. Test and examinations results are also used to create targets for schools and give rise to league tables. (There is more detail on these and other systems in Chapters 6 and 7.)

Differences between the ways in which certain components of a system are carried out matter. Changes made in one part of a system have implications for how other parts can function. It is not difficult to point to examples of this interaction. For example, there is research evidence that

- when school accountability is based on external summative assessment data, this impacts on the way that teachers conduct their own internal summative assessment and on how they use assessment formatively (see for example Pollard et al., 2000);
- how teachers carry out formative assessment can influence their own internal summative assessment practice (Black et al., 2003);
- how moderation of teachers' judgments is carried out can affect the evidence they gather and report about students' achievements (Donnelly et al., 1993).

Often unwanted effects in one part of the system on another arise from piecemeal changes in policy that ignore the relationship of parts within the whole. These interactions, and those between assessment and the curriculum and teaching methods (pedagogy), are indeed at the heart of arguments made here for change in systems where student assessment is largely based on tests.

Before embarking on making these arguments, however, we take a closer look at the components and clarify some of the terms used in describing the various ways in which these can be carried out.

Components of an Assessment System

The components of a system can be described in terms of combinations of the variables set out in Figure 1.1 under seven headings: purpose, use, type of task that provides evidence, who makes the judgment, the basis for judging the evidence, the way in which the results are reported and any moderation procedures that are needed. Some of the main variables in relation to these seven aspects are also indicated in Figure 1.1. (A far more detailed taxonomy of just one type of assessment, summative assessment by teachers, was developed by Wilmut, 2004.)

The variables in Figure 1.1 can be used to describe whole systems, as well as particular types of assessment within them. For example, the profile of these aspects for formative assessment (assessment for learning) would be:

Purpose formative
Use helping learning
Type of task regular work and some tests/tasks created by the teacher
Agent of judgment teacher and students combined
Basis of judgment criterion-referenced (detailed and task specific) and student-referenced
Form of report or feedback comment or oral feedback.

Moderation does not apply to formative assessment, but in the case of the focus of this book – assessment of learning – all seven headings do apply and Figure 1.1 makes clear the very large number of ways in which assessment for this purpose can be carried out using different combinations of the variables. Not surprisingly, how this is done matters and has a considerable impact on those involved, quite apart from any reaction to the result of the assessment. The choice of variables and how they are combined has implications for what evidence is included (validity), the accuracy of the result (reliability), the impact on those involved, and the cost of the operation in time and other resources. These four properties will be briefly discussed later in this chapter, but also revisited throughout the book as they underpin the main arguments for reform in assessment policy.

First we look briefly at each of the seven aspects in Figure 1.1 and in particular at the different ways in which they can be put into practice in summative assessment.

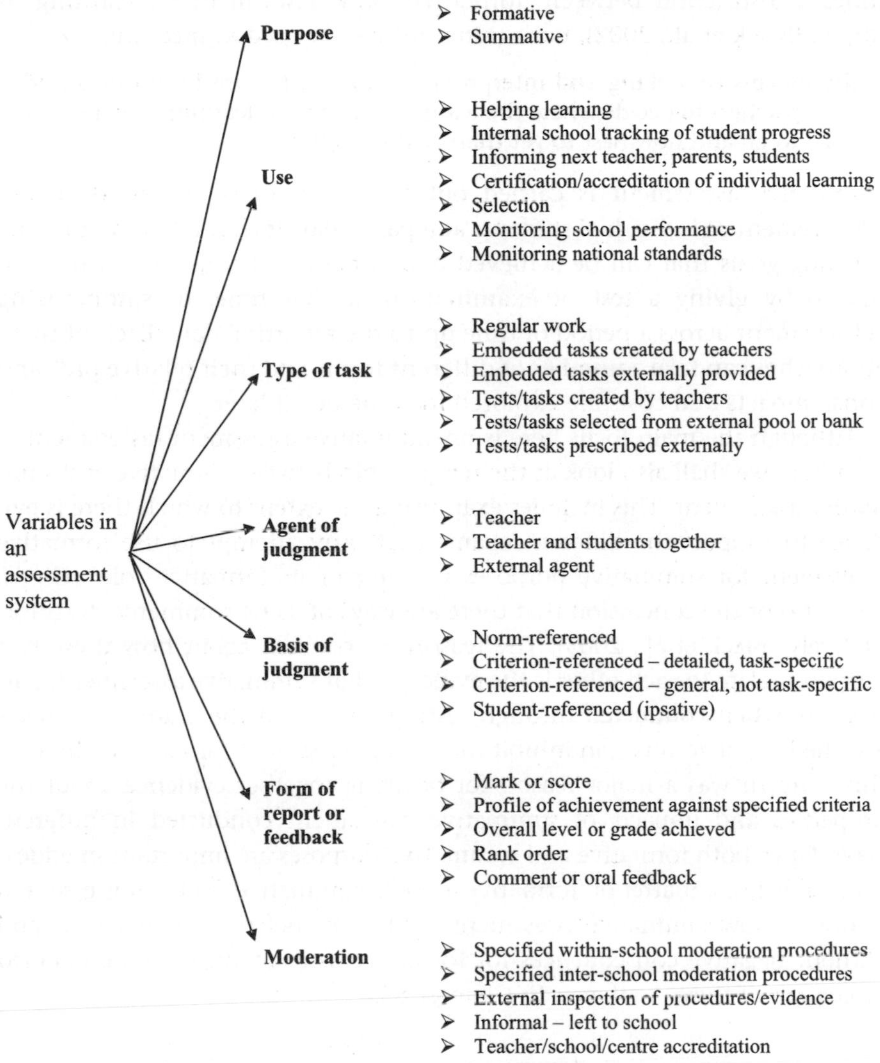

Figure 1.1 Components and variables of an assessment system

Purposes of Assessment

There are two main purposes for assessing students: to inform decisions about learning experiences and to report on what has been achieved. 'Formative' means that the assessment is carried out in order to help learning. It is detailed and relates to specific learning goals. It is essentially part of an approach to teaching and learning in which information about what students have achieved is used to inform decisions as to how to make progress. For this reason it is also called 'assessment *for* learning' and although sometimes a distinction between 'formative' and 'assessment *for* learning' is forged (Black et al., 2002), both terms are widely used as meaning:

> the process of seeking and interpreting evidence for use by learners and their teachers to decide where the learners are in their learning, where they need to go and how best to get there. (ARG, 2002b)

Summative assessment is carried out for the purpose of reporting the achievement of individual students at a particular time. It relates to broader learning goals that can be achieved over a period of time. It can be conducted by giving a test or examination at that time, or summarizing achievement across a period of time up to the reporting date. Each of these approaches can take a number of different forms and their relative pros and cons, impacts and costs are explored in some detail later.

Although the main focus here is on summative assessment (assessment *of* learning), we shall also look at the relationship between formative and summative assessment. This includes examining the extent to which there is evidence to support the different claims that 'Any attempt to use formative assessment for summative purposes will impair its formative role' (Gipps, 1994: 14) or the conclusion that there are ways of using summative tests formatively (Black et al., 2003). The reason for concern about how these two purposes relate to each other is the evidence that summative assessment, particularly when conducted through testing and when there are high stakes attached to the results, can inhibit the use of assessment formatively. Indeed, this concern was a major reason for bringing together evidence about the properties and impacts of summative assessment conducted in different ways. Since both formative and summative purposes are important in education – it is not a matter of 'formative, good', 'summative, bad' – it is essential to discuss how summative assessment can be conducted most effectively and without negative consequences for formative assessment. (A more detailed discussion of these matters is in Chapter 8.)

Use of Assessment Results

For formative assessment there is one main use for the data – to help learning. Indeed, this use defines formative assessment and if the information about students' learning is not used to help that learning, then the process cannot be described as formative assessment. By contrast, the data from summative assessment are used in several ways, some relating to individual students and some to the aggregated results of groups of students.

For individual students, the uses include reporting to parents, other teachers, tracking progress, and selection, certification or accreditation by an external body. These can be grouped under two main headings of 'Internal' and 'External' to the school community:

- 'Internal' uses include using regular grading, record keeping, informing decisions about what courses to follow where there are options within the school, reporting to parents and to the students themselves.
- 'External' uses include certification by examination bodies or for vocational qualifications, and selection for further or higher education.

In addition to these uses, which relate to making judgments about individual students, results for groups of students are used in evaluating the effectiveness of the educational provision for students. The main uses of aggregated results are

- Accountability – for the evaluation of teachers, schools, and local authorities, although the extent to which this should depend on measures of students' achievement is problematic.
- Monitoring – within and across schools in particular areas and across a whole system for year-on-year comparison of students' average achievements, but whether aggregated individual data are the most useful is contested.

In both cases, there are issues about using the results of individual students in these ways. Information yielded is restricted and does not meet the needs of users. (We return to these matters in Chapter 9.)

Type of Task

In theory, anything that a student does provides evidence of some ability or attribute that is required in doing it. So the regular work that students do in school is a rich source of evidence about the abilities and attributes that the school aims to help students develop. This evidence is, however, unstructured and varies to some degree from class to class, or even student to student. These differences can lead to unfairness in judgments unless assessment procedures ensure that the judgments made are comparable and equivalent work is assessed in the same way. One way to avoid this problem entirely is to create the same conditions and tasks for all students, that is, to use tests.

Testing is a method of assessment in which procedures, such as the task to be undertaken and often the conditions and timing, are specified. Usually tests are marked (scored) using a prescribed scheme (protocol), either by the students' teacher or external markers (often teachers from other schools). The reason for uniform procedures is to allow comparability between the results of all students, who may take the tests in different places. Just as assessment can be qualified according to the type of task, so tests are described as 'performance', 'practical', 'paper-and-pencil', 'multiple choice', 'open book', and so on. More formal tests, leading to a certificate or qualification, are often described as examinations.

Teachers regularly create their own tests for internal school use; in other cases they are created by an agency external to the school. Tests are criticised on a number of points, considered in more detail in Chapter 4, but it is the emotional reaction of many students to them that is a considerable cause of concern. The test items are unknown and students have to work under the pressure of time allowed. This increases the fear that they will 'forget everything' when faced with the test; the anticipation is often as unpleasant as the test itself. To counter this, and also to assess domains that are not adequately assessed in written, timed tests or examinations, assessment tasks may be embedded in normal work. The intention is that these tasks are treated as normal work. It may work well where the use is internal to the school, but the expectation of 'normality' is defeated when the results are used for making important decisions and the tasks become the focus of special attention by teacher and students. One example here is the coursework element of GCSE examinations, which has been the subject of critical review (see the example at the end of this chapter and Chapter 6).

Since tests and examinations are forms of assessment, the broader term, 'assessment', is used here when referring to all forms. There is a problem, however, in distinguishing testing and examinations from other methods of assessment, such as on-going assessment by teachers. Some authors attempt to identify assessment as different from testing but then fall into the trap of referring to assessment as a general category, as in 'assessment in schools', thus meaning all kinds including tests. To avoid this, the term 'assessment' will be qualified as 'assessment by testing' or 'teachers' on-going assessment' where there is any risk of ambiguity.

Agent of Judgment

The role that teachers can take in summative assessment varies from collecting evidence required and marked by external agencies (as in administering external tests and examinations) to themselves collecting evidence of, and making judgments about, the achievements of their own students. In between there are various ways in which teachers can be involved, for example in writing and marking examinations, moderating others' judgments and collecting evidence as prescribed by external agencies that is then assessed by others. Consequently the term 'teachers' assessment' can be interpreted in different ways – and the term 'teacher assessment' is even more ambiguous.

The definition of teachers' assessment used here is

> The process by which teachers gather evidence in a planned and systematic way in order to draw inferences about their students' learning, based on their professional judgement, and to report at a particular time on their students' achievements. (ARG, 2006: 4)

This draws attention to the process being no less 'planned and systematic' than alternatives using tests or tasks. Judgments have to be supported by evidence which can be gathered over time from regular work, accumulated in the form of a portfolio of particular kinds of work, or intermittently from project reports, or from specified assignments, or from occasional tasks such as fieldwork or presentations. The reference to 'their own students' emphasises that the meaning is restricted to those situations where teachers assess their own students and exclude the marking of other students' work (apart, that is, from what is involved in moderating other teachers' judgments).

Basis of Judgment

Making a judgment in assessment is a process in which evidence is compared with some standard. The standard might be what others (of the same age or experience) can do. This is norm-referencing and the judgment will depend on what others do as well as what the individual being assessed does. In criterion-referencing the standard is a description of certain kinds of performance and the judgment does not depend on what others do, only on how an individual's performance matches up to the criteria specified. In student-referenced or ipsative assessment a student's previous performance is taken into account and the judgment reflects progress as well as the point reached. The judgments made of different students' achievements are then based on different standards, which is appropriate when the purpose is to help learning but not appropriate for summative purposes.

Summative assessment is either criterion-referenced or norm-referenced. Criterion-referencing is intended to indicate what students, described as having reached a certain level, can do. But using criteria is not a straightforward matter of relating evidence to description (Wilmut, 2004). For example, the level descriptions of the National Curriculum assessment comprise a series of general statements that can be applied to a range of content and context in a subject area. Not all criteria will apply to work conducted over a particular period and there will be inconsistencies in students' performance – meeting some criteria at one level but not those at a lower level, for instance. Typically the process of using criteria involves going to and fro between the statements and the evidence and some trade-off between criteria at different levels, all of which involve some value judgments. Agreement among practitioners will then depend on the extent of shared experience, understanding and values. There may also be some comparison of the work of different students, thus introducing an element of norm-referencing in the interpretation of criteria.

Whilst 'best fit' is used in the National Curriculum assessment and in the teacher-assessed elements of the GCSE, in vocational education the student must meet every criterion in order to obtain an award at a particular level.

In the interests of clear-cut judgments the criteria are detailed, which tends to lead to a somewhat mechanistic approach to assessment, and to learning that is shallowly directed at 'ticking off' particular criteria, rather than adopting a more holistic approach (see Chapter 6).

Form of Report

The form of report depends to a large extent on the nature of the task, the basis for judgment and the audience for the report. Numerical scores from tests are a summation over a diverse set of questions and so have little meaning for what students actually know or can do for the same total can be made up in many ways. Scores also give a spurious impression of precision, which is very far from being the case (see Chapter 4). Converting scores to levels or grades avoids this to a certain extent, and also serves to equalize the meaning of a level from year to year in examinations such as the GCSE and national tests, where new items are created each year. When scores change from year to year, this could be because of differences in the difficulty of items or changes in the students' achievements. The boundary scores for grades or levels can be adjusted to account for differences in item difficulty, but this introduces a severe problem of how to decide the 'correct' cut-off score between one grade and the next. Ultimately this depends upon judgment and there is a variety of procedures (often hotly contested) for making these judgments. Black (1998) gives a useful account and critique of some of these methods and their consequences in the national debates about standards.

Scores can be used directly to rank order students, but this is really only useful in the context of selection. Again, a position in a rank order gives no indication of meaning in terms of learning. In theory, reporting against criteria which describe levels or grades can do this, but since a single overall grade or level would have to combine so many different domains as to make it almost meaningless a profile is needed. The shorthand of levels, as used in reporting National Curriculum assessment can be useful for in-school reporting, but for reporting to parents and students the levels need to be explained or replaced by accounts of what students can do.

Moderation

Moderation is generally associated with assessment where teachers make judgments of students' work, although in its wider meaning it has a role in those parts of all types of assessment where decisions are made and have to be checked. Its purpose can be quality control, or quality assurance, or both. There are several different approaches, each with advantages and disadvantages. To anticipate the discussion in Chapter 5, the main methods for quality control are statistical moderation, inspection of samples, external examinations appeals and group moderation. For quality assurance of the process rather than adjustment of the outcome, methods include defining criteria, providing exemplification, accrediting schools, centres or individuals, visits by verifiers and group moderation. In the case of teachers' assessment, as defined above, the purpose is to align the judgments of different teachers and the most appropriate methods are those that address both quality control and assurance.

The rigour of the moderation process that is necessary in a particular case depends on the 'stakes' attached to the results. Where the stakes are relatively low, as in internal uses of summative assessment, within-school moderation meetings are adequate, whilst inter-school meetings are needed when the results are used for external purposes. However, the use of exemplification can be seen as a substitute for moderation meetings, thus reducing opportunities for inter-school discussions and for the professional development that these meetings can provide.

Properties of Assessment

Whilst the components and variables set out in the last section offer a means of analytic description of assessment procedures and systems, in order to judge how effective they are for their purpose they need to be evaluated in terms of required properties.

One obvious property is that any assessment should be valid for its purpose, that it assesses what it is intended to assess. Another is that it should provide reliable or trustworthy data. But there are also other matters to be taken into account; in particular, and in view of the interdependence of the various system components, the impact on other assessment practices and on the curriculum and pedagogy. Further, there is the use of resources; assessment can be costly, both in terms of monetary resources and students' and teachers' time.

Thus assessment for any purpose can be evaluated in terms of the extent to which it meets the requirements of its uses for validity and reliability, positive impact, and good use of resources. As we will be referring to these properties frequently throughout the book we consider them briefly here, first individually and then looking at the interactions among them.

Validity

In this context validity means how well what is being assessed corresponds with the behaviour or learning outcomes that it is intended should be assessed. This is often referred to as 'construct validity'. Various types of validity have been identified, most relating to the type of evidence used in judging it (for example, face, concurrent, content validity), but there is general agreement that these are contained within the overarching concept of construct validity (Messick, 1989; Gipps, 1994). The important requirement is that the assessment concerns all aspects – but only those aspects – of students' achievement relevant to the particular purpose of that assessment. Including irrelevant aspects is as much a threat to validity as omitting relevant aspects. Thus a clear definition of the domain being assessed is required, as is adherence to it.

Reliability

The reliability of an assessment refers to the extent to which the results can be said to be of acceptable consistency or accuracy for a particular use. This may not be the case if, for instance, the results are influenced by whoever conducts the assessment or they depend on the particular occasion or circumstances at a certain time. Thus reliability is often defined as and measured by the extent to which an assessment, if repeated, would give the same result.

The degree of reliability necessary depends on the purpose and use of an assessment. When assessment is used formatively, it involves only students and teachers. No judgment of grade or level is involved, only the judgment of how to help a student take the next steps in learning, so reliability is not an issue (see Chapter 8). Information is gathered frequently by teachers who will be able to use feedback to the student to correct any mistaken judgment. However, high reliability *is* necessary when the results are used by others and when students are being compared or selected.

Impact

Here impact means the consequences of the assessment, often referred to as 'consequential validity' (Messick, 1989). It concerns the inferences drawn from the assessment information in relation to the uses that are made of it. As noted earlier, assessment generally has an impact on the curriculum and on pedagogy, which is greater the higher the stakes attached to the outcomes of assessment, so it is important that any potential adverse effects are minimized. Assessment can only serve its intended purpose effectively if this is the case. The impact is likely to be greater the more frequently summative assessment is carried out. Often teachers mistakenly assume that more summative assessment is needed than is actually the case. In particular, when there are external tests many teachers will feel under pressure to spend time preparing and practising for them, thus making what ought to be an infrequent occurrence into a frequent one.

A key factor in determining the degree and nature of the impact of student assessment is the use of results for the evaluation of teachers, schools and local authorities. The evidence for this is considered in Chapter 9 which also suggests how the most serious impacts can be avoided.

Resources

The resources required to provide an assessment ought to be commensurate with the value of the information to users of the data. The resources may be teachers' time, expertise and the cost both to the school and to external bodies involved in the assessment. In general there has to be a compromise, particularly where a high degree of reliability is required. There is a limit to the time and expertise that can be used in developing and operating, for example, a highly reliable external test or examination. Triple marking of all test papers would clearly bring greater confidence in the results; observers visiting all candidates would increase the range of outcomes that can be assessed externally; training all teachers to be expert assessors would have great advantages – but all of these are unrealistic in practice. Balancing costs and benefits raises issues of values as well as of technical possibilities.

Interaction Among the Properties

As just noted, the extent to which the property of reliability can be optimized is limited in practice by resources. Similarly, changes in procedures aimed at increasing validity, say by doubling the time used in testing, would increase the impact on the resource of teaching and learning time. A less obvious but key interaction is between reliability and validity. In essence it means that, in practice, an assessment cannot have both high validity and high reliability. This applies to whatever way an assessment is carried out.

Take tests, for example. No test can cover all the learning that is set out in the curriculum. What is tested can only be a sample of the curriculum goals and in order to make the test as reliable as possible, the sample will inevitably be biased towards those aspects that can be consistently marked or marked by machine. This favours items assessing factual knowledge and the use of a closed item format, as opposed to items requiring application of knowledge and the use of more open-ended tasks. The consequent limitation on what is covered in a test affects its validity; increasing reliability decreases validity. Attempts to increase validity by widening the range of items, say by including more open-response items where more judgment is needed in marking, will mean that the reliability is reduced.

The same arguments apply to the use of teachers' judgments instead of tests for summative assessment. Whilst validity can be high, since the data can include all outcomes, reliability will be low unless effective moderation procedures are applied (see Chapter 5). Attempts to increase reliability by standardizing the tasks that are assessed by teachers lead to narrow, artificial tasks of low validity. Black et al. (2004) describe a stark example of this in science:

> It is ironic that the only aspect of science that is entrusted, at GCSE level, to teachers' assessment has led to 'investigations' which the various external pressures have reduced to stereotyped exercises that are widely recognised to be of no interest to students and to present them with a mockery of scientific enquiry. Similar damaging effects of moderation that lead to 'rubric-driven instruction' have been reported in other subjects and in other countries. (Paechter, 1995; Baker and O'Neil, 1994) (Black et al., 2004: 5).

In recognition of the interaction of validity and reliability it is sometimes useful to refer to the combination of the two as *dependability*. The definition of this term used here gives priority to validity, so that it is taken to mean 'the extent to which reliability is optimised while ensuring validity'.

2 Assessment and the curriculum

The chapter begins by considering what information we want assessment to provide about students' learning. We note a considerable amount of official support for changes in the curriculum that would better provide for the needs of students in a world that is rapidly changing. The arguments focus on the importance of helping students to develop various 'literacies' – meaning a broad understanding of concepts in each area that enables effective engagement in modern life – such as creativity and economic productivity, citizenship, learning with understanding and learning how to learn.

We argue that the absence of representation of these goals in the information provided by many current assessment systems is partly to blame for inhibiting the real changes in educational practice that are needed. Yet the assessment of these important goals is possible and some brief examples have been indicated. The major change, however, is to move away from traditional assessment methods based on tests and to make more use of teachers' judgments. Evidence and arguments for this course of action are discussed in Chapter 4.

Introduction

What is assessed influences what is taught and how it is taught, and hence the opportunities for learning. The relationship between assessment, the curriculum and teaching methods (pedagogy) is often represented as a triangle, as in Figure 2.1, to show that each one of these has some relationship with the other two.

Of course this simple representation does not indicate the direction of the effect of one feature on another. Does the assessment influence the curriculum or the curriculum influence the assessment? Is the curriculum that students experience the same as the intended curriculum? Similar questions apply to assessment and pedagogy, for what teachers do in the classroom is

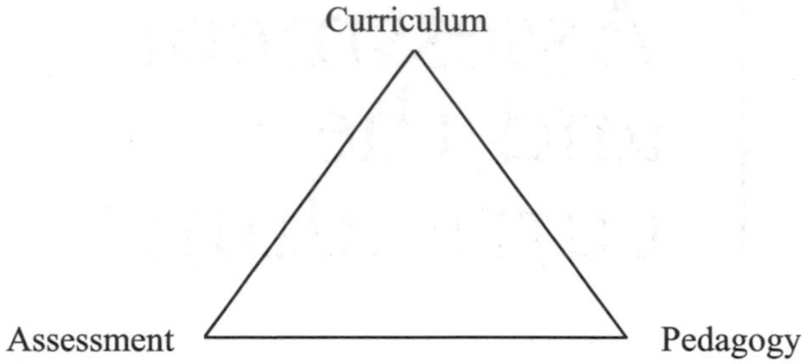

Figure 2.1 The interactions between assessment, curriculum and pedagogy

not always what they would like to be able to do (James and Pedder, 2006). Ideally we would like to think of assessment and pedagogy following the curriculum, so that methods of teaching and the assessment of outcomes are chosen to be appropriate to what we want our students to learn. Unfortunately, there are several reasons why we do not find this in reality and this can have serious implications for students' learning.

Some of these reasons follow from the uses made of the results, especially when these include judgments that affect the future of students or the status of teachers, schools and even countries, giving the assessment results what has been described as 'high stakes'. Although high stakes can be attached to the results of assessment conducted by teachers, when results are used for evaluation they invariably are derived from tests because of their supposed precision. Thus the testing itself as well as the use of the results increases the impact on the curriculum, on learning and on teaching. We return to these matters in Chapter 9 but in this chapter the focus is on the relationship between assessment and the curriculum; what we ought to assess and whether current arrangements enable us to do it.

The concern is with the substance, not the form of the assessment, yet there is evidence that the form of traditional methods continues to restrict what is assessed. The first consideration ought to be about what we want to assess and this will be the starting point here. There is ample support for new goals in education related to preparing young people for life in modern society. Yet when we come to ask whether these goals are reflected in students' school experience, the answer is not encouraging. One important reason for this is that they are not being assessed. The second part of the chapter looks at some of the difficulties of assessing these goals and what is needed to overcome these problems. This is the start of making a case for greater use of teachers' assessment.

What We Ought to Assess

A key question is, how consistent are current assessment procedures and content with a curriculum that is needed to prepare students for modern life? Current thinking, world-wide, emphasises the importance of developing in students types of skill, attitudes, knowledge and understanding that are regarded as more important than accumulating large amounts of factual knowledge. Content knowledge can be found readily from the information sources widely available through the use of computers and especially the internet. What are needed are the skills to access these sources and the understanding to select what is relevant and to make sense of it. So we need to provide students with an understanding of broad, widely applicable concepts and the ability to use them to solve problems and make decisions in new situations. This is often expressed in terms of becoming 'literate' in relation to different subject areas.

Facing new problems will be the normal run of things rather than the exception in the future lives of young people, as changes in technology affecting everyday life occur at an increasing rate. Dealing with problems responsibly involves a broad understanding of society and democratic processes and some experience in participating in them. Being able to manage change, and do more than respond to problems, requires creativity and enterprise. Further, underlying all attempts to prepare students for meeting change confidently is the need for them to learn with understanding and to learn how to learn.

It is not new to suggest that these are important outcomes of a modern education. Reference to them abounds in official documents and in reports and recommendations from a number of influential groups and councils. The questions we now need to raise are: how well are these aspects reflected in the way that students' achievements are assessed? What changes would be needed to make sure that they are included and dependably assessed? One thing is sure – if they are not included in the assessment, then the attention they receive will not match the rhetoric of their importance. Before considering how they might be assessed, however, we need to take a closer look at what these aspects are, why they are important goals of learning and what kinds of experiences promote their development.

The Development of 'Literacies'

The notion of being 'literate' has for some time been extended beyond the ability to read and write. The term now generally carries the connotation of being able to engage effectively with different aspects of modern life. So it is common to refer to 'technological literacy', 'mathematical literacy', 'scientific literacy', even 'political and social literacy'. Being literate in these various respects indicates having the knowledge and skills that are needed by everyone, not just those who will be specialists in or will make a career using knowledge of one of these areas.

The emphasis is not on mastering a body of knowledge but on having, and being able to use, a general understanding of the main or key ideas in making informed decisions and participating in society. Literacy, used in these ways, does not mean reading and writing *about* technology, mathematics, science, and the like. Rather, it means having the understanding and skills to participate in the discussion of issues and to make decisions in the many matters of everyday life that involve technology, science, politics and so on.

What this means in practice is spelled out in relation to scientific literacy by Millar and Osborne (1998), who recommend that 'the science curriculum from 5 to 16 should be seen primarily as a course to enhance general "scientific literacy"' (p. 4). They explain that this means

> that school science education should aim to produce a populace who are comfortable, competent and confident with scientific and technical matters and artefacts. The science curriculum should provide sufficient scientific knowledge and understanding to enable students to read simple newspaper articles about science, and to follow TV programmes on new advances in science with interest. Such an education should enable them to express an opinion on important social and ethical issues with which they will increasingly be confronted. It will also form a viable basis, should the need arise, for retraining in work related to science or technology in their later careers. (Millar and Osborne, 1998: 4)

Some empirical support for this view of what should be taught in science was provided by one of four research projects undertaken by the Evidence-based Practice in Science Education (EPSE) Research Network, part of the ESRC's (Economic and Social Research Council) Teaching and Learning Research Programme. Twenty-five 'experts', representing the main 'stakeholder' groups in science education, took part in a three-stage Delphi study. The outcome showed considerable agreement among all groups on the most highly rated themes (Millar et al., 2006). These were grouped under three headings:

- Nature of scientific knowledge (tentative nature of science; historical development);
- Methods of science (hypothesis and prediction; diversity of scientific thinking; creativity; science and questioning);
- Institutions and social practices in science (co-operation and collaboration in development of scientific knowledge).

A similarly broad and applied view underpins the OECD's PISA (Programme of International Student Assessment) definition of mathematical literacy as

> An individual's capacity to understand the role that mathematics plays in the world, to make well-founded mathematical judgments and to engage in mathematics, in ways that meet the needs of that individual's current and future life as a constructive, concerned and reflective citizen. (OECD, 1999: 41).

It is not difficult to see that working with such goals in mind is different from seeing science and mathematics (and history, politics and economics) as a succession of facts or algorithms to be learnt, with no attention to the overarching coherence between concepts and their relevance in students' current and future lives.

Creativity and Economic Productivity

In 2001 the Department of Trade and Industry (DTI) joined with the Department for Education and Employment (DfEE) in England in producing a paper entitled 'Opportunity for All in a World of Change'. It made a case for school education giving more attention to development of the skills and attitude needed in business and industry.

> People who generate bright ideas and have the practical abilities to turn them into successful products and services are vital not just to the creative industries but to every sector of business. Our whole approach to what and how we learn, from the earliest stages of learning, needs to adapt and change in response to this need. Academic achievement remains essential but it must be increasingly delivered through a rounded education which fosters creativity, enterprise and innovation ... (DTI and DfEE, 2001: para 2.11)

The emphasis on the need to change 'what and how we learn' underlines the links between curriculum and pedagogy, for qualities such as 'creativity' cannot be 'taught' in the same way as, say, the 'basics' of reading and arithmetic. Rather, creativity, innovation and enterprise are best engendered in schools when teachers and management practise them in their planning and provision (Hargreaves, 2003). Instead of following 'top-down' approaches, such schools develop and test out methods of providing opportunities for students and teachers to discuss, collaborate, link with other schools and local industry and use technology in teaching and learning.

Citizenship

Some of the aims, and ways of working towards them, to develop citizenship overlap with those just discussed. Citizenship includes social and moral responsibility, community involvement and political literacy, according to the DfES's Citizenship website. Again, the ways of working needed to help students achieve these aims mean enabling them to participate in, and not just learn about, links with the local community and the wider world outside school. These require students not only to learn about their neighbourhood and social and political structures, but to become involved in service to the community and to take responsible care of the environment. Through this they develop 'self-confidence and socially and morally responsible behaviour both in and beyond the classroom, towards those in authority and towards each other' (DfES, Citizenship website).

Learning with Understanding

Understanding occurs frequently in the expression of learning goals, but rarely is its meaning clear and the complexity of the concept acknowledged. Taken seriously, the development of understanding has strong implications for curriculum content and pedagogy, as do the aims of developing enterprise and citizenship. Understanding is quite different from knowing facts, although it requires factual knowledge, as White points out:

> [understanding] is a continuous function of a person's knowledge, is not a dichotomy and is not linear in extent. To say whether someone understands is a subjective judgement which varies with the judge and with the status of the person who is being judged. Knowledge varies in its relevance to understanding, but this relevance is also a subjective judgment. (White, 1988: 52)

Different dimensions and levels of understanding also have been identified, for example by Wiske who considers three dimensions related to the form of communication and four levels of depth of understanding: naïve, novice, apprentice and master (Wiske, 1998: 180). Understanding shows in the ability to organize knowledge, to relate it actively to new and to past experience, forming 'big' ideas, much in the way that distinguishes 'experts' from 'novices' (Bransford et al., 1999). Big ideas are ones that can be applied in different contexts; they enable learners to understand a wide range of phenomena by identifying the essential links ('meaningful patterns' as Bransford et al. put it) between different situations without being diverted by superficial features. Merely memorizing facts or a fixed set of procedures does not support this ability to apply learning in contexts beyond those in which it was learned. Knowledge that is understood is thus useful knowledge that can be used in problem solving and decision making.

Learning How to Learn

An important part of preparing young people for life and work in the rapidly changing society of today and tomorrow is to help them develop awareness and understanding of the process of learning – a key aspect of meta-cognition. Throughout their lives they will have to make more choices than those who lived in past decades and both work and leisure will involve activities that we can as yet only guess at. This is underlined by the OECD, who point out that:

> Students cannot learn in school everything they will need to know in adult life. What they must acquire is the prerequisites for successful learning in future life. These prerequisites are of both a cognitive and a motivational nature. Students must become able to organise and regulate their own learning, to learn independently and in groups, and to overcome difficulties in the learning process. This requires them to be aware of their own thinking processes and learning strategies and methods. (OECD, 1999: 9).

The ability to continue learning throughout life is acknowledged as essential for future generations and thus it has to be a feature in the education of every student. Since learners have to be prepared for meeting the challenge of learning anew throughout their lives, they need to learn how to learn. *Learning how to learn* is not the result of being taught to use a set of higher-order skills, but rather of having used a set of effective learning practices and applied them in various contexts (Black et al., 2006a). It is important that learning how to learn is seen as integral to, and a consequence of, effective learning. What is required for understanding learning is, therefore, no more than helping students to think about and reflect on their learning as part of the learning process. Thus meta-cognition is seen as being embedded in learning processes and is developed, as with other learning, through interaction and discussion with other students and the teacher. Learning collaboratively provides students with feedback and scaffolding that supports their understanding of learning as well as requiring and developing other skills related to problem solving and communication. Hargreaves (2007) suggests that collaborative learning and its assessment improve performance in traditional examinations.

Learning about how to learn and the ability to reflect on the adequacy of what one knows is the key to taking steps towards further learning. Research, such as that reviewed by Black and Wiliam (1998a), shows that the ability to take effective action results from students being helped to:

- see how to improve their work, by feedback that is non-judgmental;
- try to explain things rather than just describe them;
- take some responsibility for assessing their own work, finding the errors in their own or a partner's work;
- talk about and justify their reasoning;
- understand the goals and the quality of work they should be aiming for.

These are key features of using assessment to help learning (formative assessment or assessment for learning). It follows that an important requirement for summative assessment is that it supports and does not inhibit the practice of formative assessment (see Chapter 8).

Can These Goals Be Assessed?

Returning to the initial statement at the start of this chapter – that what is taught is influenced by what is assessed – raises some unavoidable questions. Are these widely advocated components of a modern education reflected in what and how we assess? If not, why not? There are three points to make in relation to these questions before tackling a further one. Can anything be done about it?

First, we can dismiss any doubt that assessment does influence teaching. More and more research studies are confirming this, the latest being a series carried out by the Learning How to Learn project (James et al., 2006). Evidence from 1,500 staff in 40 primary and secondary schools in England led to the conclusion that there is no doubt that teachers are teaching to the tests their pupils have to take; they feel they cannot do anything else. Case studies revealed that teachers believed that 'there are circumstances beyond their control which inhibit their ability to teach in a way they understand to be good practice' (Marshall and Drummond, 2006: 147).

Second, it is not difficult to see from what is assessed in external tests and examinations the extent to which the skills, understanding and attitudes just discussed are included. The result is 'hardly at all'. Since teachers' internal assessment tends to emulate the external assessment, this also fails to reflect these important goals. There is no suggestion here that only these goals should be assessed, for it is important to know whether students have the knowledge and basic skills that underpin the development of broad concepts and the different forms of literacy. But it is essential that all valued goals are included in assessing students' progress. At present this is not the case in systems such as that in England.

Third, in relation to the reasons for this neglect, some points made in Chapter 1 are relevant at this point. For assessment where the results are used beyond the school, tests are preferred to other forms of assessment because they are considered to be reliable and to be 'fair'. In fact the assumption of 'fairness' is not justified (see Chapter 4), but leaving that aside and focusing for the moment on the measured reliability on items, it was noted (p. 26) that tests are preferred because they are viewed as having higher reliability than other forms. However, tests are only as reliable as the scoring or marking and steps taken to make reliability as high as possible favour items that are closed, so that marking depends as little as possible on human judgment. Clearly, items that require students to be creative or to present arguments or show understanding of a complex situation do not fit this description. Consequently they are rarely considered and would be unlikely to survive the pilot trials used in developing and selecting items for external tests and examinations.

What is Possible

It is legitimate to ask at this point whether it is indeed possible to create test items that assess application, problem solving, critical thinking, and so on. Perhaps surprisingly the answer is positive – but with a caveat. Some items of these kinds were included in surveys conducted nationally, by the Assessment of Performance Unit (APU) in England, Wales and Northern Ireland in the 1980s, and such items currently feature in the National Assessment of Educational Progress (NAEP) in the United States. International surveys of the OECD's PISA are wholly concerned with the assessment of scientific, mathematics and reading literacy. For example, the item in Figure 2.2 was created as part of a bank to assess scientific literacy by the PISA.

In the APU, the skills of enquiry were assessed through individual practical investigations as in the example in Figure 2.3.

These examples, dealing with real things or real data, are highly dependent on the choice of content. The surveys in which they are used provide the evidence that students who perform well in one item will not necessarily do so in another item testing the same skills but in a different context. In a recent carefully-designed study in the USA, Pine et al. (2006) assessed fifth grade students using several 'hands-on' performance tasks, including one based on 'Paper Towels' (as in Figure 2.3) and one called 'Spring', about the length of a spring when different weights were hung on it. They found 'essentially no correlation for an individual student's scores. Students with either a 9 or a 1 Spring score had Paper Towels scores ranging from 1 to 9' (Pine et al., 2006: 480). For particular tasks selected from a wide range of possible tasks, the 'task sampling variation', is large and this means that to obtain a reliable score for an individual student would require that individual to tackle a totally unacceptable number of tasks.

For individual students the tasks have high validity but they are low on reliability and fairness, since a student's score is highly dependent on the nature of the tasks chosen. However, in a survey where students are sampled it is indeed possible for a large number of tasks to be given, since any one student takes only a sample of the total items and tasks. The scores of individual students in these surveys are not relevant and become meaningful only when combined with those of other students in the sample.

Although extended performance or practical tasks seem particularly prone to the task sampling variation, there is an element of this problem in every test for individual students since these can only contain a sample of possible items.

Read the following information and answer the questions which follow.

WHAT HUMAN ACTIVITIES CONTRIBUTE TO CLIMATE CHANGE?

The burning of coal, oil and natural gas, as well as deforestation and various agricultural and industrial practices, are altering the composition of the atmosphere and contributing to climate change. These human activities have led to increased concentrations of particles and greenhouse gases in the atmosphere.

The relative importance of the main contributors to temperature change is shown in Figure 1.

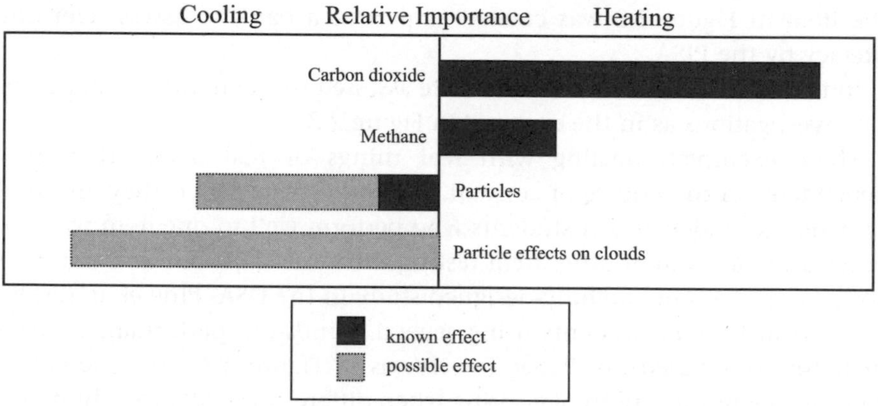

Figure 1: Relative importance of the main contributors to change in temperature of the atmosphere. Source: adapted from http://www.gcrio.org/ipcc/qa/04.html

Bars extending to the right of the centre line indicate a heating effect. Bars extending to the left of the centre line indicate a cooling effect. The relative effect of 'Particles' and 'Particle effects on clouds' are quite uncertain: in each case the possible effect is somewhere in the range shown by the light grey bar.

Figure 1 shows that increased concentrations of carbon dioxide and methane have a heating effect. Increased concentrations of particles have a cooling effect in two ways, labelled 'Particles' and 'Particle effects on clouds'.

Item 1:
Use the information in Figure 1 to support the view that priority should be given to reducing the emission of carbon dioxide from the human activities mentioned.

Item 2:
Use the information in Figure 1 to support the view that the effects of human activity do not constitute a real problem.

Figure 2.2 An item used in the PISA assessment of Scientific Literacy (OECD, 2000)

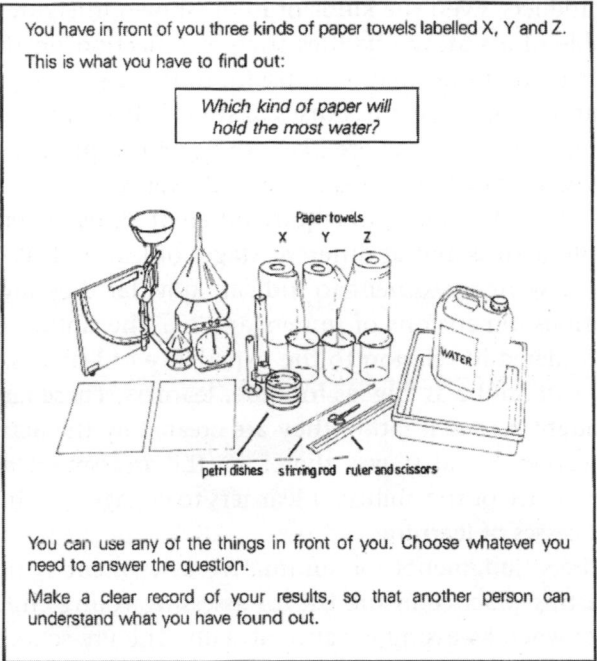

You have in front of you three kinds of paper towels labelled X, Y and Z.

This is what you have to find out:

Which kind of paper will hold the most water?

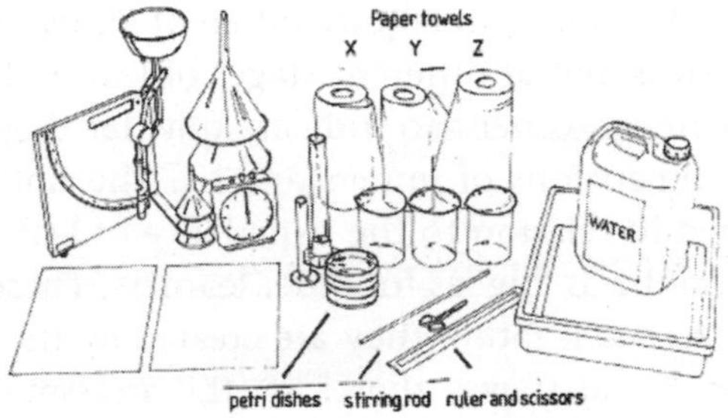

You can use any of the things in front of you. Choose whatever you need to answer the question.

Make a clear record of your results, so that another person can understand what you have found out.

Figure 2.3 The Paper Towels investigation in the APU (Welford et al., 1985)

Alternatives to Tests

Since valid and reliable assessment of some of the achievements that ought to be assessed comes up against some unavoidable obstacles, are there any alternatives for summative assessment? Fortunately there are, all of them depending on the fact that the experience that students need in order to develop the desired skills, understanding and attitudes also provides opportunities for their progress to be assessed. The key factor is the judgment of the teacher. Assessment by teachers can use evidence from regular activities supplemented if necessary by evidence from specially devised tasks introduced to provide opportunities for students to use the skills and understanding to be assessed.

Over the period of time, such as a semester or half year, for which achievement is being reported, students have the opportunity to engage in a number of activities in which a range of attributes can be developed. These same activities provide opportunities for the development to be assessed by the teacher. In other words, the limitation of the restricted time that a test provides does not apply when assessment is teacher-based.

Methods of assessment based on observation during regular work also enable information to be gathered about processes of learning rather than only about products. Even the kinds of items shown in Figures 2.2 and 2.3 are not capable of assessing qualities such as reflection on the process of learning. This kind of information is useful to those selecting students for advance vocational or academic courses of study, where whether candidates have learned how to learn and are likely to benefit from further study is as important as what they have already learned. Nor is assessing understanding a simple matter, it is likely to require different kinds of evidence in different curriculum areas and at different stages of learning. When students are learning we want assessment to indicate how far they are progressing along the various dimensions of understanding. The notion of 'big' ideas has to be considered in relation to the experience of learners; for younger learners they will not be as 'big' as for older learners. These larger concepts cannot be 'taught' as such, rather they are created by the active participation of the learner. At all stages, therefore, the assessment also needs to encompass evidence of the ability of learners to engage in using and developing the processes of learning.

Using teachers' judgments for summative assessment is not new; it is built into existing practice in the UK for assessing young children and for older students when assessing vocational skills. The Pre-school or Foundation Stage assessment includes personal, social and emotional development, physical development and creative development, as well as development in basic literacy, numeracy and knowledge of the world (see Chapter 6). These assessments serve a formative as well as a summative purpose and are not for external use, but in other countries teachers' assessment is used for important external assessment (see Chapter 7).

Ways of assessing outcomes such as orientation to lifelong learning and understanding are also available. They depend upon self-reporting by students, but since there are no 'correct' and 'incorrect' responses and no scores, there is no sense of being tested. For example, the Effective Lifelong Learning Inventory (ELLI) comprises a number of statements to which learners respond by indicating their agreement or disagreement on a five-point scale. It provides a profile of a student's characteristics relating to willingness and enjoyment of learning. It can be used with students from the age of about eight onwards. The statements have been found to relate to seven dimensions, each of which is an aspect of effective learning: changing and learning, meaning making, critical curiosity, creativity, learning relationships, strategic awareness and resilience. Examples of statements in the inventory are:

'I can feel myself improving as a learner.'

'When I have trouble learning something, I tend to get upset.'

'Talking things through with my friend helps me to learn.'

> 'I like it when I can make connections between new things I am learning and things I already know.' (Adapted from Deakin Crick et al., 2002: 51–2)

The results can be used by teachers both to identify the help that individual students may need to develop their 'learning power' and also to devise learning strategies and create a classroom climate that favours learning.

Student questionnaires have also been used by Black et al. (2006b) to explore attitudes to and views about learning. In their instrument, students respond by marking one point on a six-point scale between pairs of statements. For example, in some cases this is pairs of opposites:

I enjoy learning	( ) ( ) ( ) ( ) ( ) ( )	I don't enjoy learning

and in other cases, non-exclusive pairs:

I like to be told exactly what to do	( ) ( ) ( ) ( ) ( ) ( )	I like to do things where I can use my own ideas

Black et al. (2006b) found inconsistencies when the questionnaire was completed for a second time by the same students. These were considerable for the younger students (ten year olds) in their study, which the authors suggest may have been in part 'an inevitable effect of immature response to questions that address issues and generalizations which are too novel for them' (Black et al., 2006b: 167). This indicates that there are limitations in using self-response methods with younger students when the concepts involved are not easily expressed in simple language.

Hautamäki et al. (2005) have created the Finnish Learning-to-Learn Scales, which have been widely used in research in Finland and also translated into Swedish and English. There are scales assessing cognitive skills and competencies, beliefs, motivational orientations, self-regulation, self-concept in academic areas, self-worth and self-esteem. High values of reliability are reported for these scales. Validity, however, will depend upon the extent to which they predict how students behave when, as adults, they are faced with situations where they have to apply their learning of how to learn.

In the next chapter we will continue to focus on what ought to be assessed by considering what those who receive and use assessment say about what they want to know about students.

3 Views of 'users' of assessment

This chapter looks at how assessment and different assessment procedures are viewed by the users of assessment information – parents, students, teachers, higher education and employers.

The evidence gathered about parents shows that they are more concerned about receiving information that they can use to help their children than about how it is gathered. Both they and students want a wide range of learning within and outside schools to be reported. Like parents, students are distrustful of assessment by teachers being used for important summative purposes. Students appear to regard tests and examinations as a necessary if not helpful part of their school experience, particularly in a context where testing dominates the curriculum. It appears, however, that greater knowledge about the process of assessment, about the criteria used and about quality assurance procedures could reduce the suspicion of teachers' judgments.

Teachers themselves lack confidence in other teachers' judgments. Research shows that there is often a gap between what teachers would like to do in their classroom assessment and what they are able to practise. The gap is greatest in relation to practices that would help students to develop responsibility for their learning and reflect on how they learn, giving students less opportunity to work towards these widely-advocated goals. Indeed, it is information about whether students are likely to be able to learn and take responsibility for it that is needed by both employers and higher education in order to select students who will benefit from further study or training and stay the course.

Introduction

How are assessment and different assessment procedures perceived from the point of view of the 'users' – parents, students, teachers, higher education and employers? In particular, do they currently receive the information about students' achievements that is of most value to them and how do they view current assessment procedures and the impact these have on students' education? This chapter continues the discussion of whether current assessment practices meet the needs of those involved in using information about individual students.

Parents, students and teachers are receivers of both internal and external summative assessment, whilst employers and higher education receive only results meant for use external to the school. Some users have definite views about how the information should be obtained and communicated; for others how the assessment is carried out is less important than what is included or excluded. The points made here draw on evidence from several sources including an ASF seminar attended by students, a representative of a parents' organization, a senior administrator of an awarding body for vocational qualifications, a director of admissions at a leading university and researchers who have carried out studies of students' and parents' views of assessment.

Users' Views

Parents

In relation to 'internal' summative assessment an enquiry into parents' views was carried out in Scotland through a series of 'Open Space' meetings. (Open Space meetings are organized around a theme, but thereafter the agenda is in the hands of participants, who raise the issues of greatest concern to them and what they feel appropriate actions might be in terms of these issues. Priorities are established by voting on all the issues and actions.) It was found that parents were least concerned about how their child compared with others or with overall standards and most concerned about how to collaborate in helping their child's progress. Five key themes emerged across the meetings. These were:

- The focus for parents was effective learning, for example 'learning for life', 'skills to improve learning' and 'learning holistically'. The purpose of assessment was to facilitate this. Parents were interested in teachers (required by the schools and the system) identifying their children's strengths and areas that needed developing in an ongoing way. They saw this as key to their children progressing and being successful learners.
- Parents wished to know well in advance what their children were going to be learning in different aspects of the curriculum and the targets their own child would be working towards.
- They wanted partnership – a real dialogue about what their children needed to do to improve and how they could help with this. They wanted their children fully involved in these conversations too.

- Parents also wanted good and regular communication about their children's progress via a range of media – and they wanted it at points early enough in the session to allow them to work with schools to resolve any obstacles to learning their children were experiencing.
- From the centre (Education Authorities/Scottish Executive) they wanted support for assessment for learning practices, not more tests. (Hutchinson and Pirie, 2005)

An informal enquiry into the views of parents in England, reported at an ASF project seminar (see ASF Seminar 5 on the ARG website), largely accorded with the Scottish results for internal assessment. In relation to external assessment, parents were aware of the effects it can have on the curriculum and on students' motivation, particularly the lower achievers. As in Scotland, parents' views on the curriculum were linked to their views on assessment. They wanted children to have a wider range of experiences and for out-of-school learning to be recognized. They wanted a greater range of achievements to be included in national tests. They thought that students would benefit more from assessment by teachers as opposed to external testing and that this would support students' motivation and self-esteem. Whilst some distrust of teachers' judgments was reported, it was thought likely that this could be alleviated by providing more supporting evidence and communicating the criteria used in assessment.

Students

Research in relation to students' views of summative assessment is limited, as most studies focus on their views of the curriculum and conditions of learning. For example, the study by McIntyre et al. (2005) of how teachers use students' ideas about how to improve classroom learning and teaching reported only comments about how they engaged with content. The students were invited to talk about what they did or did not do that could help their learning, which might be expected to give an opening to talk about assessment, but no comments of that nature were reported. Perhaps these (mainly lower secondary) students did not recognize assessment as being something that related to learning.

A study carried out in Northern Ireland found that by the age of 16 students were aware that the curriculum was dominated by what was needed to gain the necessary results to enter higher education. These students took the instrumental view that this was necessary, despite admitting that what they were doing was not particularly useful in its own right for their future lives. Lower-attaining students saw their test results as a sign of their ability, whilst higher-attaining students saw tests as showing them how they could improve. Towards the end of secondary school, students liked tests and examinations and they were concerned about the fairness of project work and impressionistic marking of course work. Students liked tests because they gave a clear-cut measure of progress based on 'right or wrong', enabled them to see their strong and weak points, made them revise for examinations and were good practice for 'real' examinations. In a system dominated by examinations, what students wanted was help in passing them.

It appears that when examinations dominate the curriculum and pedagogy, as has been the case in Northern Ireland for many years, students tend to focus on what is needed to pass them and do not consider alternatives. Evidence reported from Scotland, where examinations do not dominate daily experience so much, showed that students were more concerned with greater variety in their learning experiences. At Open Space events held for pupils in Scotland the questions raised and discussed by pupils mainly concerned the content of the curriculum, how they learned best and actions relating to dress codes. Pupils wanted more lively teaching (and teachers), more variety and alternatives for study, less 'teacher talk', and more encouragement to do their best at whatever level they had reached.

Direct evidence from two students from a school in England, who attended the ASF seminar (see ASF Seminar 5, ARG website) echoed the views of parents in relation to the use of teachers' judgments. They thought that there would be bias in their teachers' judgments, that depending on them would impose an extra strain on teachers and that 'all staff mark differently'. However, they also recognized that the advantage would be that teachers could take the context of work into account, and that with strong, clear criteria and teacher collaboration in using the criteria, bias could be minimized. They recalled an experience of having to mark their own work and being given the criteria, as being 'fantastically helpful'. Similarly they could identify the pros and cons of testing, recognizing that tests impose too much pressure, cause cramming, and detract from the enjoyment of education. They were also aware that current summative assessment did not give them credit for life skills, such as being able to talk to a roomful of academics, education administrators and senior teachers!

A typical example of examination-dominated school experience was reported by a school student from London, writing in *The Independent* on the day of receiving his AS level results (17 August 2006). He wrote of the examination process:

> This process would be fine if it was reflecting the work that was done by students, rather than shaping what and how is taught to them. Exam preparation, and increasingly education, is now about adapting to this system; forcing an examiner ... to give you that top grade. Students are drilled to jump through hoops that the examiner is holding. Exam preparation is part of education – but they shouldn't be one and the same thing. (Tom Greene, 2006: 35)

Teachers

Teachers are both providers and users of assessment data. When asked what they want their pupils to have learned, the list includes being independent and self-critical learners, good problem solvers, thoughtful citizens, effective communicators, able to work in groups, as well as having basic skills and curricular knowledge and understanding. Yet information about this learning is not included in either internal or external tests. Only at the Foundation Stage, where formal testing is not possible, are some of these included in information given and received by teachers (see Chapter 6 for information about the Foundation Stage Profile).

As receivers of information, teachers notoriously distrust the information they receive from other teachers, preferring to use their own judgment. This applies particularly to judgments based on work across a course, but also to test scores when there is suspicion of intense coaching to pass tests. So why do teachers think their own judgments are to be trusted, but other teachers' are not? The answer may lie in the use of test results to set targets for teachers and schools to meet, often with sanctions attached to missing the targets. In these circumstances, each teacher needs to maximize the test levels of students when they leave their class or school. Any inflation in these levels makes it more difficult for the next teacher to show that they can improve scores. It also means that teachers feel they must prioritise meeting targets for tests results ahead of encouraging wider learning that they actually value.

In other words, teachers know that their own and therefore other teachers' judgments are influenced by the use made of the results. Clear evidence of the circumstances that contribute to this situation is reported by James and Pedder (2006) from a survey of 558 teachers in England. The teachers were from primary and secondary schools and were among those having little or no managerial responsibility in their schools. The survey instrument comprised a number of statements about assessment practice. For each statement teachers were asked to respond in two ways: first about their practices, indicating whether the statement was 'never true', 'rarely true', 'often true' or 'mostly true' in their case, and second about their values in relation to each statement, saying whether it was something that was 'not at all important', 'of limited importance', 'important' or 'crucial'. From the results it was possible to identify differences between teachers' practice and what they valued in relation to classroom assessment.

The most highly-valued practices, rated as important or crucial by a high percentage of teachers, were:

> Practices that generate evidence for the teacher of learning that influences planning, that encourage discussion and clarification of learning objectives, purposes and assessment criteria with students, and that involve open ques-

> tioning, formative feedback and an emphasis on task involvement.
> Teachers also placed high value on assessment practices that provide opportunity for students to assess their own learning, to develop independence in their learning, to engage constructively with mistakes and problems, to build on their strengths, to view effort as an important component of learning and to think critically about their learning. (James and Pedder, 2006: 119, item references omitted)

When percentages of teachers valuing each statement were compared with the percentage indicating that they were often or mostly true in their practice, marked gaps were revealed. The greatest gaps (25 per cent or more) were in relation to:

- teachers regularly discussing with students ways of improving learning how to learn;
- students being helped to think about how they learn best;
- students being given opportunities to decide their own learning objectives;
- students being helped to plan the next steps in their learning;
- students being given opportunities to assess one another's work.

Although the focus of the study was the practice of assessment rather than the content, nevertheless these results indicate the kinds of information that were valued but not often included in classroom assessment. To help students learn independently requires information beyond that about what they know and can do in relation to the prescribed curriculum. Yet only 46 per cent of teachers often helped students to plan the next steps in their learning, whilst 83 per cent valued this activity.

It seems that the situation in which teachers do not trust each others' judgments arises from the same pressures that narrow the focus of their own assessment to factual knowledge and inhibit the use of assessment to develop students' capacity for reflection on learning and their ability to take greater responsibility for their learning. Developing greater confidence in teachers' judgments is essential if we are to see more attention being paid to the development of competences that are important for continued learning throughout life. Only if these goals are assessed will they be given serious attention.

Experience of systems and sectors which depend to a large extent on assessment by teachers suggests that this can be achieved through greater openness and competence in the process of assessment and recognition that teachers can provide the information that is needed about important aspects of learning beyond those covered by tests. Openness requires that evidence and the criteria for judging it are available to all and that teachers have the opportunity to challenge and reconcile differences of judgment through moderation processes. These increase their understanding of the process and their confidence in their own and others' judgments.

Higher Education

The information required by those selecting students for higher education is not just about what the students have achieved but whether they will stay the course and benefit from university study. Examination results do not give this information, partly because of the nature of the examination and partly because, as the earlier quote from a student shows, many students have learned how to pass examinations rather than how to be become independent learners likely to succeed in the different environment of higher education.

Despite recognizing that examination grades are of dubious validity and reliability, universities that attract the highest performing students are looking for finer distinctions within the top grade, by identifying A* and A** and so on performance. Technically this makes little sense and dissatisfaction with advanced-level grades means that more universities resort to setting their own examinations, only adding to students' pressures. Rather than take this route, there is an opportunity for a revised system, based to a greater extent on moderated and dependable teachers' assessment to provide the information that would be really helpful to universities. Evidence from an extended project carried out by a student, for instance, is likely to give more relevant information than high marks on tests and examinations that could be affected by cramming. Universities are well aware that many students have spent years 'chasing grades'.

Information about students' study processes and skills is often supplied to universities by teachers, but teachers' reports on students are in general not trusted, since schools are anxious to promote their students' chances of admission. However, where a school is known to the admissions tutors and a relationship has been established, then the school reference is more likely to be used. Teachers can, in these circumstances, supply evidence and honest opinions about whether a student is likely to stay the course and has learned how to learn. What is needed is greater transparency in the assessment process; for schools to be more honest with their students about their abilities in relation to what is needed for university study, so that unrealistic expectations are not built up. With greater openness, there ought to be more self-assessment and self-selection.

Employers

Employers, as in the case of higher education tutors, want to be able to select those who will be able to do the job. In recognition that traditional examinations don't give this information, an alternative system has been devised. It is in this area of vocational studies that the emphasis on validity has led to assessment on the job by the teacher, trainer or employer.

Learners can obtain qualifications at various levels according to when they are judged, by the teacher or trainer or trained work-place assessor, to be meeting various competence requirements.

Detailed specification of competence criteria guides the assessment; meeting these criteria comprises both the training and the evidence of competence. In work-place assessment the employer is the trainer and the assessor, both the source of assessment information and the user of that information. Thus emphasis is on validity and authenticity, the role of awarding bodies being to focus on the extent to which procedures have been correctly implemented (quality assurance) rather than on moderating decisions (quality control).

The on-going assessment can be formative, in identifying where skills still need to be improved, as well as summative. Learners who are not successful initially in meeting the criteria can try again and be assessed as many times as required until they succeed. However, unlike an examination such as GCSE, which can be passed without success in all parts, it is necessary to meet all the relevant criteria in order to be awarded a vocational qualification.

The award of National Vocational Qualifications (NVQs) in England is carried out by approximately 150 bodies linked to different occupations and involves a somewhat complex system of moderation to ensure reliability as well as validity (more details of NVQs are given in Chapter 6). The assessment conducted by the assessor working with the learner (level 1) is moderated by an internal verifier (level 2), who in turn is moderated by an external verifier on behalf of the awarding body (level 3), the whole process being under the surveillance of the Qualifications and Curriculum Authority (QCA). Different bodies carry out these functions in other parts of the UK.

Despite the complexity, this assessment process is judged to be working well. Adding a written test as part of a vocational qualification had been found to be associated with an increase in drop-out rate. The key to a successful operation is the training given to the assessors and to frequent reviewing and improvement in the system to maintain its validity and operational viability. Learners and teachers are both aware of the criteria and therefore self-assessment is a feature at all levels in the assessment and moderation processes.

Comment on Users' Views

It appears that, while parents, teachers, students and higher education admission tutors are not satisfied with the information they obtain from tests and examinations, they have difficulty in accepting alternatives based on teachers' judgments. The reasons for this focus on the suspicion of inflation in grades and levels, particularly when targets are set in terms of the results achieved by students. It is evident that overcoming mistrust of teachers' judgments requires greater transparency in procedures, including moderation, and openness among all concerned about judgments and how they are arrived at. This view is supported by the practices used in the assessment of vocational skills, where all involved are aware of the criteria to be met and where procedures are carefully monitored.

The often aired view of employers and college and university tutors that many students lack initiative and basic learning skills is a different but not entirely separate matter. When these qualities and competences are not assessed in schools, they are not represented in the curriculum experience of students. The survey by James and Pedder (2006) shows that this is not because teachers don't value these and other qualities, such as learning how to learn, but they feel constrained by the external tests and examinations to focus almost entirely on what is to be assessed in them. We need what is assessed to become more consistent with what is valued and with important learning outcomes; this must involve some change in the methods of assessment.

4 Evaluating assessment methods

This chapter attempts to bring together arguments and evidence from research, where it is available, to evaluate the 'fitness for purpose' of assessment conducted in different ways. The criteria for evaluation are the four properties of validity, reliability, positive impact and level of required resources. The formative purpose of assessment is included in the discussion in preparation for later consideration of the relationship between summative and formative assessment (see Chapter 8). Summative assessment for internal use is considered separately from summative assessment for external use, although several points apply to both. In each case, the validity, reliability, impact and resources required are compared when the assessment is carried out through testing and examinations and through using teachers' judgments. There are pros and cons in relation to each approach, summarized in table form on p. 63, but on balance the evaluation supports a case for making more and better use of summative assessment by teachers. The main disadvantage is found in the reliability. So, in Chapter 5, we look at what can be done to improve the reliability and trustworthiness of teachers' judgments.

Introduction

In Chapter 1 four key properties of assessment were identified as ones that need to be considered in making decisions about how to assess students for particular purposes and uses of the data. These properties – relating to validity, reliability, impact and required resources – can also be used as criteria for evaluating existing assessment procedures in relation to 'fitness for purpose'. The assumption is that an assessment procedure that is fit for purpose is one which provides results of the most appropriate levels of reliability and validity, has only those impacts that are wanted, and makes best use of resources.

In this chapter we evaluate methods of conducting assessment in relation to these criteria. Although the focus of this book is summative assessment, it is useful to include formative assessment in this discussion. This is partly because formative assessment is essentially 'close to the learning' and provides an example of how evidence can be obtained from students' learning experiences. In addition, consideration of the properties of formative assessment sets us up for a later discussion of the relationship between formative and summative assessment (see Chapter 8).

Formative Assessment

In formative assessment, evidence is gathered during learning activities and interpreted in terms of lesson goals. Some notion of progression in relation to a goal is needed for this interpretation, so that information about where students are in this progression can be used to indicate what next steps are appropriate. Evidence of current learning is fed back into teaching and learning to help students take these next steps. This feedback helps to regulate teaching so that the pace of moving toward a learning goal is adjusted to ensure the active participation of students. Students can participate in these processes if teachers communicate to them their goals for the lesson and the criteria by which they can judge their progress towards the goals. The lesson goals may well vary in detail for different students according to their previous experience and progress in their learning.

Validity

For formative assessment to have high construct validity the evidence that is collected and the criteria by which it is judged must relate to the intended learning of a specific lesson. Thus the criteria will be task specific and considerably more detailed than for summative assessment. For example, a lesson goal might be for students to find out in what places and conditions particular living things (snails, squirrels, bluebells, roses, and so on) are to be found. The longer-term goal is the understanding that living things are generally found in habitats to which they are suited. So, for formative assessment the teacher would be picking up evidence about what the students are noticing about the particular living things being studied and about the places in which they are found. From this (s)he will judge whether to spend more time discussing and observing these situations or to move on to more challenging interpretations of observations that can lead to achieving long-term goals. No doubt another lesson goal will be for students to develop the necessary skills of observation, and the interpretation of evidence and information about this, too, will be used to regulate progress towards more detailed observation and systematic interpretation by the students.

For optimum construct validity, the methods that are used have to provide information that is related to the learning goals and is interpreted in relation to progression in development of overarching concepts or skills. The methods a teacher uses to gather the information in this situation are likely to be a combination of direct observation, including listening to students' discussion, and review of what they write or draw about their experiences.

Reliability

Reliability, or accuracy, is clearly a desirable property of any assessment information, but it is not necessary to be concerned about the reliability of formative assessment information because it is gathered frequently and the teacher will be able to use feedback to correct for a mistaken judgment (see Chapter 8). In the example just cited, if the teacher judges some students as being ready to move towards a generalization about living things and their habitats, but what they do subsequently shows that this is not the case, then further experience of particular living things can be provided. The problem here lies in the adequacy of the evidence that the teacher uses and this can be corrected by gathering a better sample of evidence.

Even though we can say that reliability is not an issue in formative assessment, it is clear that the more carefully any assessment is made, the more value the information will have in helping learning. To anticipate a point to be made later, the action needed to improve the reliability of information based on teachers' judgment for summative assessment will inevitably also influence the reliability of the judgments they make for formative purposes.

Impact

A positive impact on teaching and learning is the overall purpose of formative assessment. Thus the evaluation of the effectiveness of formative assessment must be made on the basis of whether or not further learning of the kind anticipated has taken place as a result. In some cases it may be possible for teachers and students together to decide on immediate action. For example, if a teacher finds some students' ideas about an event they are investigating in science are not consistent with the scientific explanation, it may be possible for the teacher to help the students to set up a test of their ideas and so see for themselves the need to consider alternative explanations. In other cases, the teacher may take note of what is needed and provide it at a later time. The point here is that the evidence is used to inform decisions about helping further learning.

At the same time, not all learning is of equal value; any impact ought to promote valued learning. This leads to the question: can there be learning that is not valuable, that is 'out of keeping with social priorities', as

Hargreaves (2007) puts it? Indeed there can be, if we think of learning that might lead to intolerance of minorities or habits that endanger health. In a rather less extreme case, we might say that learning *only* by rote is also out of line with social priorities since it does not lead to the life-long learning that is so widely recognized as now being needed by all. Rote learning has a place in education for some learning outcomes, but we would not value an education that left the impression that learning is all about receiving and memorizing information. The nature of formative assessment, discussed in Chapter 8, makes it particularly relevant and indeed necessary for learning with understanding.

Evidence of the positive impact of formative assessment on learning has been provided by Black et al. (2003), based on work with secondary teachers of mathematics, English and science, whose students achieved 'significant learning gains' following the use of assessment for learning. Black et al. (2003) also cite research by Bergan et al. (1991), White and Frederiksen (1998) and a review of research by Fuchs and Fuchs (1986) as providing evidence of better learning when formative assessment is built into teaching. The positive impact of non-judgmental, 'no marks' feedback on students' levels of interest, effort and achievement is reported in studies by Butler (1988) and Brookhart and DeVoge (1999), while studies by Schunk (1996) have found positive impacts on achievement of self-assessment.

A particular point arising from the Fuchs and Fuchs (1986) review of research was that the greatest gains resulted when teachers took care to review information about students and to use it systematically to guide their teaching. Formative assessment is a complex combination of interconnected practices and positive impacts may not result if teachers are following procedures mechanically without understanding their purpose. For example, Smith and Gorard (2005) reported that when some teachers put comments but no marks on students' work (a key feature of formative assessment), these students made less progress than others given marks. However, the comments written by the teachers did not supply guidance on how to improve the work and so deflect students' attention from how well they had done. It is essential for teachers to embrace the change in teacher–student relationships that is involved in implementing formative assessment. Without this change, students will not use feedback to improve their work or openly reveal their understanding and difficulties as is necessary for assessment to be used for learning.

Resources

The running costs of methods used in formative assessment are zero. Once formative assessment methods are implemented, class time is used differently; attention is focused on developing students' understanding, which may mean that more time is needed for a particular topic when its study is informed by formative assessment compared with superficial 'delivery' of information. But there are 'upfront' costs in providing the professional development required. In particular, while assessment theoretically can be used to help learning in relation to all goals, teachers need help in the form of descriptions of progression in various aspects of learning. Further, some good examples are needed to help teachers and students use evidence to identify next steps.

Summative Assessment for Use Within the School

Summative assessment for internal purposes is, by definition, under the control of the teacher, within the limits of the school's policy on assessment. The information is required for keeping records of the progress of individual students, reporting to parents and students at regular intervals, passing information to other teachers on transfer from class to class, or guiding decisions about subjects for further study. The evidence may be gathered from regular work, or special tasks, teacher-made tests or externally-developed tests, and from students' self-assessment. Although the evidence from these sources can be used to provide feedback to students and into teaching decisions, the main reason for collecting it is to check up on what students have learned from a series of lessons over a period of time. For these judgments, the evidence is compared with criteria that are the same for all students.

Validity

This will depend on how well the evidence used reflects the learning being assessed. Teacher-made tasks and tests designed specifically for assessment purposes frequently focus rather narrowly on knowledge and information gained rather than the full range of learning goals, such as attitudes, problem-solving ability and creative and critical thinking skills. This usually happens because teachers emulate externally-devised tests in creating their own.

Construct validity is likely to be greater when teachers use evidence from regular activities, as these should cover the complete range of goals. Moreover, evidence can then be collected and used for formative assessment and later reinterpreted against common criteria (Harlen, 2006b, and see Chapter 8). On the other hand, the validity of information from teachers' assessment depends on the extent to which the evidence actually gathered is a good sample of work in the areas concerned. Moreover, if these areas are not well covered in the implemented curriculum, the opportunity for assessment is clearly limited.

Use of external tests is less likely to provide information of higher construct validity for internal purposes than teachers' assessments, due to a poorer match of external tests to the learning goals over the relevant period (unless, that is, what is taught is reduced to what is tested, which would seriously neglect important goals). A combination of tests and on-going assessment by teachers will not increase validity, for there can be no doubt that what is tested will be taught and so using tests will not extend the range of evidence beyond what can be gathered through assessment of regular work anyway. However, there are other reasons for combining tests and teachers' judgments (discussed in Chapter 9).

Reliability

As noted in Chapter 1, for all assessment where both reliability and validity are required to be optimal, there is a trade-off between these two properties. In the case of tests or examinations, striving for reliability can infringe construct validity, since in their development there is a preference for items relating to those outcomes that are most reliably assessed, commonly those requiring factual knowledge and answers that can be marked unequivocally. The selection process tends to exclude what is more difficult to judge, such as application of knowledge, critical reasoning and affective outcomes.

In the case of summative assessment for internal purposes the trade-off can be in favour of validity, since no terminal decisions need hang on the reported data. This would suggest that, from the arguments given above, use of teachers' judgments based on the full range of work is to be preferred. It has the further advantages over using tests, in that it avoids sources of unfairness due to the particular selection of items and the reaction of individual students to tests. If the evidence is derived from regular work and is gathered over a period of time, it covers a range of opportunities for students to show their learning without the anxiety associated with tests.

However, threats to reliability need to be minimized. To increase the reliability of teachers' judgments, some internal school procedures for teachers to moderate each others' judgments are necessary. The situation is that teachers will each be making judgments about a diverse, but different, range of work that was not completed under the defined conditions that apply in tests. Moreover, teachers have access to other information about students, such as their general behaviour and attitudes, which can introduce 'noise' into the system. Hence, if the teachers working within the same assessment system in a single institution are to ensure that their judgments are consistent with each other, there will need to be internal moderation procedures.

This is likely to involve teachers of the same subjects or age groups meeting together to align their judgments of particular sets of students' work, representing the 'latest and best' evidence on which the record or report is to be made. Internal school meetings to consider and align judgments of specific pieces of work will also improve teachers' use of evidence and criteria in their formative assessment and give rich feedback on their own teaching (see Chapter 5).

Impact

The impact of internal summative assessment on students depends not only on what information is gathered and how, but also on how assessment tasks are presented, how frequently students are graded and the range of information that is taken into account in arriving at a grade. In relation to how assessment tasks are presented, Brookhart and DeVoge (1999) make the point that exhorting students to work 'to get a good grade' is on the one hand motivating to students but on the other sets up 'a performance orientation that ultimately may decrease motivation' (p. 423). They suggest that teachers should make a point of encouraging students to find satisfaction in the work and value its usefulness for further learning.

On the matter of frequency of assigning grades, levels, or making formal reports, unwanted consequences for students' motivation of internal summative assessment can be reduced by not doing this more frequently than is really necessary. Exceeding requirements for reports at key points in a year by assessing students in terms of levels or grades more frequently means that the feedback that students receive is predominantly judgmental and encourages students to compare themselves with others. This much is clear from research studies of classroom assessment. For example, Pollard et al. (2000) found that when teachers became focused on assigning levels in their assessment, this affected how they responded to students. In such circumstances there is little attention to the formative use of assessment. Unintended consequences are likely to be minimized by using evidence from regular activities, interpreted in terms of reporting criteria on a 'latest and best' basis and doing this only when summary reports are required and not more frequently.

The impact of internal assessment is also related to what is taken into account in giving a grade or mark. Studies of the grades given by teachers show that these are often influenced by the teachers' knowledge of students' attitudes and behaviour. This evidence is discussed further in Chapter 5 in relation to bias and errors in teachers' judgments. The relevant points here are, first, that whilst students may be aware of how teachers were grading them and so interpret their performance in similar ways to the way the grades were assigned, a study by Pilcher (1994) found that this was not the case for parents; 'parents perceived grades as reflecting their child's achievement level' (Pilcher, 1994: 83). Second, this practice amounts to using grades as rewards and punishments and not just for recording students' achievements. In other words, they are used as extrinsic motivation, incurring all the disadvantages for students' motivation for learning that this entails (Harlen and Deakin Crick, 2003).

The relationship between assessment and what is taught, and how, can be used to advantage by changing assessment methods to more fully reflect intended learning goals. This was demonstrated in a project aimed at changing the assessment practices in English and mathematics of third grade teachers in a school district in the USA, which agreed to waive standardized testing for two years in the schools taking part. Flexer et al. (1995) conducted weekly workshops with teachers to introduce them to assessing students' performance instead of the tests. The researchers reported several effects on teachers and students by the end of the first year. Teachers were using more hands-on activities, problem solving and asking students for explanations. They were also trying to use more systematic observations for assessment. All agreed that the students had learned more and that they knew more about what their students knew. The teachers reported generally positive feedback from their own classes; the students had better conceptual understanding, could solve problems better and explain their solutions. The teachers' response was to attempt further change in assessment and instruction practices and become more convinced of the benefit of such changes.

Resources

The key resources needed for internal summative assessment are the time of teachers and the learning time for students. However, the cost of purchasing commercial tests or services that provide, mark and feed back test results for this purpose can be considerable. When tests are used, students' time is occupied in taking them and in practising for taking them. If ongoing assessment by teachers is used instead students may be involved in selecting pieces of work for assessment, which is a valuable activity in self-assessment and reflection on their learning.

How much of teachers' time is spent in internal summative assessment also depends on whether tests or judgments based on regular work are the predominant source of evidence. Surveys of time spent on assessment can give a rough idea of what is involved, but need to be treated with caution. Three such surveys (QCA, 2004; SHA, 2004; Sheffield Hallam University, 2003) were used in the ASF project to make rough estimates of resources used in summative assessment in England (see ASF Working Paper 3, on the ARG website).

In primary schools there is often more use of teachers' judgments than tests and so time is needed for moderation. This is estimated as being about

30 hours per year, or just less than one hour a year per student. No massive retention of evidence is necessary since the work to be assessed exists in students' notebooks or files. The teacher, preferably with the student, can select a valid sample across the relevant goals, representing the best work. Thus the main resource cost is in teacher time. A considerable compensation, however, is the opportunity this provides for making formative use of the information as part of collecting it for the summative review and helping some students to realise that, although they may be achieving at a lower level than others, there are ways in which they can, with effort, improve (Dweck, 2000).

In secondary schools, the surveys found that teachers depend more on internally-created tests or on tests provided as part of packages of curriculum materials and spend little time on moderation meetings. The time spent on preparing and marking tests amounts to roughly 30 hours per class per year. For both secondary and primary school teachers these hours are in addition to time spent on regular marking and assessment of classwork.

Summative Assessment for Use External to the School

What has been said in the last section about the properties of summative assessment for internal school uses applies to all summative assessment, but when the results are used by those outside as well as inside the school the process requires more rigour than in the case of summative assessment for internal uses. The results may be used for selection or comparison among students from different schools and for evaluating teaching. In these uses there is an assumption that the summary grade, level or standard achieved means the same for all students, no matter who makes the judgment or how it is made. This might be taken to lead to the conclusion that, in the trade-off between validity and reliability, preference ought to be given to reliability. However, the requirements of high validity are equally as strong as for internal summative assessment. Thus the emphasis has to be on increasing reliability in the interpretation of the evidence whilst maintaining validity at the highest level possible.

Validity

High validity is essential, first because it sends a strong message about what learning is valued and second, because results of external summative assessment are often used to judge a school, even when league tables based on examination or national test results are discouraged. When decisions about their future opportunities may depend on the results of assessment for external purposes, the stakes are already high for individual students.

Adding high stakes for the teacher, by using the results for evaluation of their teaching, means that the assessment, in whatever way it is carried out, is bound to have a strong influence on teaching and learning. (This is taken further in the later discussion of impact.) The relevance to validity is that the assessment will not give the information that is needed by those receiving and using the information if it does not reflect the full range of goals but only a narrow range of outcomes that are more reliably assessed.

As discussed in Chapter 3, most users want to see evidence of both academic and non-academic achievement. Students and parents want all students' achievements, including what is learned outside the classroom, to be reported and credited; both employers and higher education admission tutors want to be able to identify students who are independent learners, who show initiative and perseverance and have learned how to learn. Reporting such outcomes when students leave school is not enough; progress towards them needs to be monitored throughout school so that necessary action can be taken. Consequently such outcomes must be included in valid summative assessment.

As in the case of internal summative assessment, evidence gathered and judged by teachers can improve the match between the range of intended learning and the information provided in the assessment, since teachers can build up a picture of students' attainment across the full range of activities and goals, as part of their regular work. This gives a broader and fuller account of achievement than can be obtained through tests, which can only include a restricted range of items and a sample of learning goals. Freedom from test anxiety means that the assessment is a more valid indication of students' achievement.

Reliability

Summative assessment for external purposes is conducted to inform decisions. These may affect individual students, as in entry to selective schools or to further or higher education courses. Even when summative assessment results do not have serious implications for individual students, they can acquire high stakes when the results are used for evaluating teaching or ranking schools. In either case, the accuracy of the information is of the essence.

Assessment by teachers has the potential for providing information about a wide range of cognitive and affective outcomes and need not define the curriculum. However, the reliability of teachers' judgments is widely held to be low and there is research evidence of bias. But the research also shows that when criteria are well specified (and understood), teachers are able to make judgments of acceptable reliability. This is a key part of the case for making greater use of teachers' judgments for summative assessment and will be considered in detail in Chapter 5.

The moderation procedures that are required for quality assurance can be conducted in a way that provides quality enhancement of teaching and learning as noted earlier. In some circumstances it may be desirable for teachers to supplement the evidence they use in making their judgments with externally-devised tasks or tests. A well-designed set of assessment tasks available for teachers to use has several benefits. Such tasks can exemplify for teachers the situations in which skills and understanding are used and thus guide them in developing their own embedded assessment tasks. They can also be of particular benefit to newly-qualified teachers and those who need to build their confidence in their ability to assess students. There are, however, disadvantages and the pros and cons will be discussed further in Chapter 9.

Discussion of what is 'acceptable' reliability is not well informed by relevant data. It is generally assumed that the information provided by tests and exams is necessarily more reliable than that derived from teachers' judgments. However, this leaves out of consideration the error that arises because tests are limited to only a small sample of the work covered and a different selection of items could easily produce a different result for particular students. For example, Wiliam (2001) and Black and Wiliam (2006) estimated that in the case of the national tests at age 13 in England, even if the measured reliability of the test is 0.85, about 40 per cent of students will be awarded the wrong grade level. When teachers' judgments are used, taking evidence from across the whole range of work, this source of misclassification is removed.

Impact

Teaching will inevitably be focused on what is assessed. The impact of summative assessment on learning experiences can be restrictive if there is a mismatch between the intended curriculum and the scope of the assessment. This is inevitable when external tests are used, for they can only assess a sample of intended learning outcomes, as just mentioned, and the more readily assessed ones at that. However, the impact on student learning experiences can be positive if the assessment is carried out so that the results reflect the full range of intended goals and if it helps to clarify the meaning of those goals.

Research shows that summative assessment based on teachers' judgments across a range of student work, rather than on specific tasks, is associated with a strong, positive impact on teaching and learning when it is built into teachers' planning and not added on to satisfy official requirements. For example, Hall and Harding (2002) and Hall et al. (1997) report that the introduction of teachers' assessment in the National Curriculum Assessment in England and Wales was perceived by teachers as having a positive impact on students' learning. This impact was enhanced by teachers working collaboratively towards a shared understanding of the goals and of the procedures to achieve these goals.

There is also evidence that older students (15 and 16 year olds) respond positively to assessment of coursework. Bullock et al. (2002) reported that students liked coursework because it provided opportunities for more independent learning, led to better retention of skills and knowledge and motivated further learning. They also thought that assessment of coursework was less pressured than examinations and enabled them to learn during the assessment process. Teachers, however, were more aware of the constraints of the assessment criteria and were often reluctant to allow students to take control of coursework. There was also evidence that teachers had not communicated assessment criteria effectively to students.

> Teachers assume that students will perceive the demands of learning and assessment in the same way that they do. In fact, despite teachers' assertions that marking schemes have been shared with students, the students tend not to understand what the assessment criteria actually require from them. Our research suggests that it is not sufficient to tell them; illustrations, examples and models are required. (Bullock et al., 2002: 338)

Several other studies also echoed this finding. For example, an earlier study by Iredale (1990) of the graded assessment in science project in the 1980s found that only a third of students even claimed to understand the scheme. Iredale also reported that the scheme, intended to replace a single, end-of-course examination with a series of school-awarded certificates throughout the five years of secondary school, though liked by some students led to others feeling pressure from the frequent testing (on average one test every four weeks). Lower-achieving students particularly were faced with constant reminders of their failure to progress.

A theme across several research studies of summative assessment is that when results are used for accountability of teachers and schools this puts pressure on teachers to increase test and examination grades, which is known to lead to teaching to the tests – giving multiple practice tests and coaching students in how to answer test questions rather than in using and applying their understanding more widely (Harlen and Deakin Crick, 2003). Validity is infringed because results no longer signify the learning achieved, but rather the ability to answer test or examination questions. Other known consequences are the de-motivation of lower-achieving students and, for all students, a view of learning as product rather than process (ARG, 2004).

Some of these consequences can equally follow from using teachers' judgments for summative assessment if the results are used for accountability. In such circumstances, moderation procedures can become over-elaborate and constrain teachers to collecting evidence using 'simple and safe' methods rather than more educationally valuable ones. Then there is likely to be a tendency to focus on a narrow interpretation of criteria and on *performance* rather than *learning*. The solution lies in a change in the way schools and systems are evaluated, a point we will return to in Chapter 9.

Resources

External summative assessment by tests and examinations is expensive, both to individual schools and to the system as a whole. Attention is given most often to the direct costs of providing, administering, invigilating, marking, and reporting tests and examinations. These costs are borne variously by the QCA, the awarding bodies, schools and colleges. According to the survey carried out in 2003 for the QCA by PriceWaterhouseCoopers (PWC) these costs total £370m for all Key Stage tests, GCSEs, AS and A levels and the assessment of various vocational skills. This figure is certainly far too low, since entrance fees increased by over 70 per cent in the subsequent three years (see the ASF conference report on the ARG website).

As noted earlier, estimating the costs of assessment is notoriously difficult; the uncertainty of concepts, the complexity of variables and the variation in practice amongst schools mean that all reports have to be treated with great caution. However, the overall estimate by PWC of overall costs, both direct and indirect, of £610m in 2003 (almost certainly an underestimate) has not been disputed. This figure includes the cost of teachers' time in the process of administering tests and examinations in pre-secondary and secondary schools in England. It is this cost in teachers' time and in uncosted student learning time that ought to be reviewed in considering resources for external summative assessment.

Some tentative estimates (ARG, 2006) for the costs in English schools indicate that the end of primary school tests mean that teachers are each year spending the equivalent of about a week of contact time on preparing and marking tests, and students about three weeks of learning time. The actual time spent on national testing is much smaller than the time spent on regular tests given by the teacher. Other evidence (for example Reay and Wiliam, 1999; Pollard et al., 2000) would suggest that this is the result of teachers giving students practice tests and using tests in preference to their own judgments. The amount of testing conducted by teachers would be expected to fall if teachers' judgments were more widely used and trusted, with teachers and students then being able to spend a significant proportion of their time in other ways.

A move to making greater use of teachers' judgments in external summative assessment means more time is needed for moderation. Since primary school teachers in general already spend 30 hours per year on moderation, any additional time needed could be accommodated by changing the use of time now spent on testing. At the secondary level, where currently little time is spent on moderation, fewer tests and more assessment by teachers would increase the need for moderation. However, the time saved in testing would more than compensate for the time necessary to provide about half a day every three weeks for moderation activities. What is needed for moderation, of course, is time out of class and this could be provided by saving on examination fees and employing extra teachers. The cost of entrance fees in one age 11–18 years school in 2006 was £400,000 (an increase of 72 per cent over the previous three years). Even if only half of this sum could be saved, it would surely enable the school to employ more staff and so allow all teachers time to make judgments based on a review of their students' work in a particular course and to participate in moderation meetings or other quality assurance procedures. We return to the matters of quality assurance, quality control and quality enhancement in Chapter 5.

Evaluation of Summative Assessment Practices

This discussion of assessment for students for various purposes, in terms of how well they meet the four criteria, has highlighted issues relating to the use of tests and teachers' judgments for summative assessment. The main points, including the pros and cons of each, are summarised in Table 4.1.

Evaluating assessment practices using criteria such as those suggested here can indicate where procedures are working well and where changes are needed to maximize fitness for purpose and minimize unintended, negative consequences.

Table 4.1 Main points from the evaluation of summative assessment practices

Evaluation criteria	Summative assessment by teachers	Summative assessment by tests
Validity	• Potential for the full range of goals reflecting the whole curriculum in each domain • Freedom from test-anxiety and from practice in test-taking means that students can show what they can do in normal conditions • Validity depends on opportunities provided in teaching	• A sample only of the full range of goals and a sample only of those goals that are assessed • Ensures that all students are judged on the same items and tasks
Reliability	• Perceived as being unreliable and biased • Judgments require moderation appropriate to the use of the data • With appropriate training can reach levels of reliability similar to those of tests	• Sampling means that a large proportion of students may be misclassified • Some external tasks or tests may be needed to ensure external confidence in comparability across schools
Impact	• Reflects and reinforces what is taught; can use evidence from formative assessment • Provides opportunities for students' self-assessment	• Leads to coaching what is tested, teaching test-taking skills, and a summative ethos in classroom assessment • Schools ensure that all students are taught what is required by the awarding bodies' specifications
Resources	• May increase teacher workload due to additional responsibilities • Training and moderation essential • Less external testing likely to mean less use of commercial tests in preparation for them • Teacher time released from preparing and marking tests • Students' learning time increased	• Takes large proportions of teaching and learning time • High cost to schools for entrance fees and for administering external examinations • Separates roles of assessor and teacher

PART 2 Using Teachers' Judgments for Assessment of Learning in Practice

5 Using teachers' judgments

This chapter concerns the question of how to improve the reliability of summative assessment by teachers whilst protecting its high validity which is one of the main reasons for preferring teacher's assessment to tests and examinations. Evidence from a systematic review of research identifies two dimensions of the process of criterion-based summative assessment as having particular significance in affecting reliability. The two dimensions are the degree of prescription of the sources of evidence or the tasks to be assessed and the detail of specification of criteria used in judging them. The research evidence and arguments lead to the conclusion that criteria that indicate a progression in the underlying skill or concept being assessed, but leave the choice of tasks to the teacher, are to be preferred to approaches that specify tasks to be assessed. The criteria are not task-specific but in their detail focus attention on relevant aspects of students' work that relate to the goals of learning.

In the second main section of the chapter we consider a range of ways to ensure quality, both in the process and in the product of assessment. Moderation approaches are compared in terms of their impact not only on the procedures and outcomes of assessment, but also on the enhancement of quality more widely in relation to teaching and learning. This leads to the conclusion that procedures that give teachers greater responsibility for the process of assessment and opportunities for group moderation of the process and outcomes are educationally most sound as well as leading to dependable assessment.

Introduction

The evaluation of assessment methods in terms of the properties required for different purposes, in the last chapter, lends considerable weight to the case for greater use of assessment by teachers. Certainly in relation to validity and the potential for providing the kinds of information about students wanted by users, assessment by teachers has considerable advantages over tests and examinations. The balance is also in that direction in relation to impact and required resources. But when it comes to reliability, assessment based on teachers' judgments is perceived as inferior to more controlled and formal methods, even though the latter are considerably less reliable than they are generally assumed to be (see page 59 and Satterley, 1994).

So what is known about the reliability of teachers' judgments and what can be done to guard against bias and inaccuracy? In the first part of this chapter we look at research into assessment by teachers. The evidence is taken from a systematic review of research conducted using the procedures and tools of the EPPI-Centre. The process includes the careful application of criteria and the selection of the most relevant studies, giving the strongest evidence relevant to the focus of review. A full report of the procedures and results can be found in Harlen (2004). The results revealed evidence of low reliability of teachers' assessment in certain circumstances. But the research also showed how the reliability of teachers' judgments can be improved and the conditions under which summative assessment by teachers can lead to fair and dependable assessment.

In the second part of the chapter, various approaches to quality control and quality assurance of teachers' judgments are outlined. These approaches are roughly compared in terms of certain aspects, including the contribution they make to quality enhancement of teaching and learning as well as to the process and dependability of assessment.

The Reliability of Teachers' Summative Assessment

The research evidence cited here was drawn together in a systematic review of research following rigorous procedures devised by the Evidence for Policy and Practice Information Coordinating Centre (EPPI-Centre). The procedures include a thorough search for research studies relevant to defined review questions, in this case referring to the evidence for the reliability and validity of teachers' assessment used for summative purposes and the conditions affecting this reliability and validity. The initial search found 431 potentially relevant studies, of which 30 were selected as specifically addressing the review questions. These studies were subject to in-depth data extraction conducted independently by two researchers, followed by reconciliation of any differences of interpretation. There were also independent judgments made of the weight of evidence provided for the review so that greater emphasis could be given to findings from the most relevant and methodologically sound research.

Before considering the evidence from the research, it is important to bear in mind certain methodological problems in studies of the reliability of teachers' assessment. A good number of such studies base their claims on how results of teachers' assessment of students' performance compare with scores in tests or examinations of the same students. But given that the reliability of tests and examinations is questionable, studies comparing grades or levels given using teachers' judgments and by tests provide dubious evidence, since neither can be assumed to be 'correct'. This situation can be avoided by looking at the internal consistency of each set of results without directly comparing them. When this is done, the difference between tests and assessment by teachers often disappears. For example, Black (1993) quotes a study by Griffin (1989) in which teachers' use of reading and writing scales was found to be as high as can be achieved with external tests.

A further methodological problem is that teachers' assessment and tests generally assess different, though overlapping, aspects of achievement. So, while not expecting perfect correlation, the question arises as to how high the correlation can be expected to be. For instance, in a study of National Curriculum assessment of 11 year olds from 1996 to 1998, Reeves et al. (2001) found that teachers' assessment and the test results agreed to an extent judged as being consistent with the recognition that they assess similar, but not identical, achievements. These authors point out that

> if the methods agree completely in nearly every case, there would be a strong argument that one or the other was redundant, while, on the other hand, if they frequently yield quite different results, this would raise serious concerns that the system contained a fundamental flaw. (Reeves et al., 2001: 142)

However, just how one arrives at the appropriate degree of agreement is not clear.

It is also useful to know that in most studies reviewed the researchers depended on questionnaires or interviews with teachers, so that the only information available about the process of how their assessment was carried out was in the form of self-reports. In some cases there was no information at all about the process used. So it is often uncertain as to what evidence was actually used by teachers, how it was gathered and how it was interpreted. In only a few cases were the actual practices observed. Where this was the case, considerable differences among teachers were found at the primary school level and between different subject teachers at secondary school level. In studies of portfolio assessment in the United States, teachers often failed to document the pieces of work selected for each portfolio and to ensure that an adequate sample of the range of work was included (Koretz et al., 1994).

Approaches to Assessment by Teachers

Summative assessment in education is a process of deciding, collecting, interpreting and communicating evidence to provide a summary of students' achievement. When considering assessment by methods that in various ways depend on the use of teachers' judgments, the main variables that define particular approaches are the evidence collected and the way in which it is interpreted and reported. Different approaches to summative assessment by teachers vary most significantly in the extent to which, on the one hand, there is specification of the sources of evidence (referred to as tasks, for convenience) and, on the other hand, specification of the criteria by which the evidence from these tasks is turned into levels, grades, scores or rankings.

Taking combinations of the extreme cases, we can describe four types of approach with the following characteristics:

- *A high level of specification of both task and criteria* This means that teachers are required to collect certain pieces of work and to base their assessment on these using sets of criteria that match the work samples. Examples are some types of portfolio assessment, where types of tasks to be included in the portfolio are closely prescribed and criteria given for each type.
- *A high level of specification of task and a low level of specification of criteria* In this approach the types of task to be judged are specified but teachers are asked to assess them with the minimum of guidance. This happens, for instance, in portfolio assessment where types of work to be included are specified and teachers rate the work in relation to the goals, such as on a five-point scale where the only guidance is 5 = high, 1 = low.
- *A low level of specification of both task and criteria* Here the teacher is given freedom to select the evidence, so the validity of the evidence is in the teacher's hands. The criteria are general and not specific to the tasks and so do not provide guidance as to what evidence is the most valid. An example here would be when teachers are asked to rate the level of students' work on a scale without further guidance as to the criteria to use.
- *A low level of specification of task and a high level of specification of criteria* In this approach the freedom to select evidence is combined with more specific, but still generic, criteria which guide the selection of work assessed. This approach is reported in a study by Rowe and Hill (1996) where sets of indicators, arranged in a sequence of developing competency, were provided for each aspect of each curriculum area assessed.

These four types are polarized versions, formed by treating as dichotomies what in reality are dimensions of variation in the specification of tasks and criteria. There is a much larger range of types described by the two dimensions in Figure 5.1.

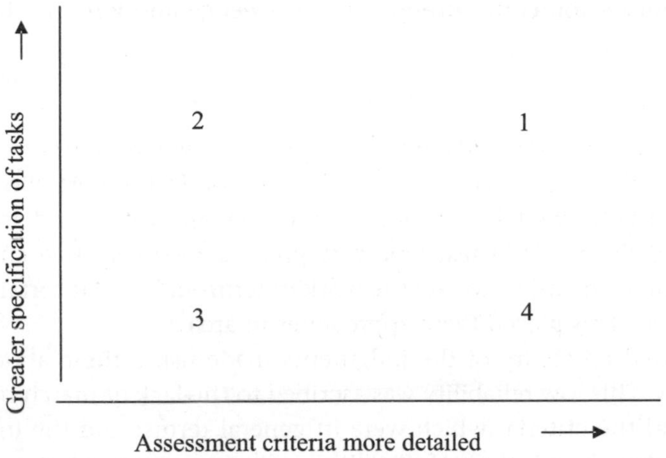

Figure 5.1 Dimensions of variables describing assessment approaches

When tasks are unspecified, tightly defined criteria can guide the selection of work assessed (area 4), whilst general, non-specific criteria leave the validity of the sample of work in the hands of the teacher (area 3). When tasks are closely specified (areas 1 and 2), the validity depends on the selection of tasks made in designing the assessment programme rather than by the teacher, and on how well the criteria match the specified tasks.

The extent to which tasks, the sources of evidence for assessment by teachers, are specified is at the heart of the reasons for including assessment by teachers in assessment systems; the more tightly specified the tasks the less opportunity there is for a broad range of learning outcomes to be included in the assessment. Moreover, it can be argued that there is little point in specifying tasks if the conditions for completing them are not also constrained, turning the class into an examination room and thus nullifying the advantages of normal work that assessment by teachers allows. In practice, conditions can be far from uniform across all students even if the tasks are tightly specified.

Area 1

Approaches to assessment in area 1, where both task and criteria are closely specified (as, for instance, in an externally-devised practical science investigation or oral assessment in a foreign language) can provide reliable data. This has been reported, for example, by Good (1988) in relation to foreign languages and Frederiksen and White (2004) in science. But in these cases, the teacher is acting as an administrator of an instrument devised by others; indeed is administering an external test. This meets the definition of summative teachers' assessment (page 18) only because the application of the criteria requires professional knowledge and could not be carried out by someone without this knowledge and who has been on the spot.

Areas 2 and 3

Not surprisingly, the dependability of approaches where neither task nor criteria are well specified has been found to be low. In the portfolio system approach initially tried in Vermont (Koretz et al., 1994) and in Texas (Shapley and Bush, 1999) teachers were given a relatively free choice of what to include and asked to rate the work in terms of how far certain goals were achieved. This placed these approaches in area 3.

The reported reliability of the judgments made using these approaches was very low. This low reliability was ascribed to the lack of match between the tasks and the criteria (which were in general terms) and the inconsistency in teachers' application of the criteria. Steps were taken to tighten the guidelines for selecting work by prescribing a 'core' set of tasks (and so moving the approach into area 2) and then adding detailed guidelines for scoring that matched the tasks, putting the approach into area 1. But even these changes were not successful in raising the reliability to a level where the measures could be used for reporting individual achievement. Further, this approach carries the risk of attention being focused on the prescribed pieces of work, just as it can be focused on what is tested by external tests, especially when the outcome is used for a purpose that has high stakes for the teachers. The selection of tasks may also infringe validity.

Area 4

Greater dependability was found in studies falling in area 4, where there are detailed, but generic, criteria that allow evidence to be gathered from the full range of classroom work. The 'subject profile' approach (Rowe and Hill, 1996) is one example here. Sets of criteria were provided relating to achievement in various subjects and in specific aspects within subjects. Rather than trying to match a particular piece of work with a particular criterion, teachers took evidence from several relevant pieces and formed a judgment on the basis of the best match between the evidence and the criteria. The criteria also served the additional function of focusing attention on the outcomes of particular kinds of work so that teachers, alerted to looking for particular behaviours, are less likely to miss them. The criteria thus guide the selection of evidence without prescribing it. Other studies (Frederiksen and White, 2004; Hargreaves et al., 1996; Shavelson et al., 1992) also suggest that when criteria are well specified, teachers are able to make reliable judgments.

In another example, the assessment by teachers in the National Curriculum Assessment in England and Wales allows evidence to be used from regular classroom work. How teachers go about this assessment has been the subject of several studies (Gipps et al., 1996; Hall et al., 1997; Radnor, 1996). These studies showed a variety of approaches but this variation does not in itself necessarily affect the reliability. Teachers vary in their teaching approaches and any less variation in assessment practice in this context would not be expected. Certainly, variation according to the nature of the subject and how it is taught is to be expected if assessment is truly embedded in regular work.

But the validity of approaches that leave the selection of tasks unspecified depends on the extent to which the evidence actually gathered is a good sample of work in the areas concerned. While criteria may lead teachers to consider work from relevant areas, if these areas are not well covered in the implemented curriculum, the opportunity for assessment is clearly limited. Consistency in applying criteria seems to depend upon teachers being clear about the goals of the work, since this influences the thoroughness with which relevant areas of the curriculum are covered in teaching (Hargreaves et al., 1996; Koretz et al., 1994). The context of the school's support and value system has also been identified as having a role in how assessment by teachers is practised (Hall and Harding, 2002). Other conditions associated with greater dependability include the extent to which teachers share interpretations of criteria and develop a common language for describing and assessing students' work.

Subject Differences

The review of research gave no evidence that assessment by teachers is more or less reliable in certain subjects rather than others. Differences between subjects in how results from teachers' assessment compare with test results were reported, but there were no systematic trends across different studies. The source of differences seemed to be the kinds of evidence used by teachers of different subjects, teachers of English making more use of classwork and mathematics and science teachers making more use of internal tests. These findings are, of course, unrelated to the issue of whether a certain level or grade has a general meaning across subjects.

Addressing Bias

While progressive criteria may provide the potential for reliable assessment, they do not assure it. Research studies give evidence of bias – a non-random source of error – due to teachers taking into account information about non-relevant aspects of students' behaviour or apparently being influenced by gender, special educational needs, or the general or verbal ability of a student, in judging performance in particular tasks. For example, general behaviour was found to influence teachers' judgments of younger students' achievements. As classroom behaviour is linked to gender in the early years of school (little girls tend to be better behaved than little boys), the result is sometimes reported as gender bias. But Bennett et al. (1993: 351) found an effect of behaviour after controlling for gender and academic ability. Those whose behaviour was poor were judged to be poorer academically, regardless of skills and gender. The effect is much less for older students. At the other end of the school age range, in a study of A level biology, Brown (1998) reported evidence that a teacher's general impression of a student's ability in the subject influenced the teacher's assessment of a project which was intended to assess distinctive skills.

Other examples could be cited and each case indicates not only the problem but points to its solution. For instance, it is evident that when everyday knowledge of students interferes with judgments, teachers are not applying criteria as intended. The problem may lie in the clarity of the criteria, the teachers' understanding of them, or how they are being used. Training can help in correcting the way criteria are applied (quality assurance) and moderation of judgments involving teachers who do not have everyday contact with the students concerned provides a check on judgments (quality control). But the underlying understanding of criteria seems to require a different approach to training. Studies by Frederiksen and White (2004), Hargreaves et al. (1996) and Rowe and Hill (1996) point to the participation of teachers in developing criteria as an effective way of enabling the reliable use of the emerging criteria.

Moderation Practice

Reference was made in several studies reviewed to various forms of moderation, including the adjustment of marks (Good, 1988), agreement across teachers (Radnor, 1996), the use of exemplars (Radnor, 1996) and the development of 'a community of practice' (Hall and Harding, 2002). Methods that depend on teachers meeting together to share their assessment of specific pieces of work require time and resources, which were supplied when National Curriculum assessment was first introduced in England and Wales, but were later discontinued. Radnor (1996) noted that secondary school teachers recognized the importance of teachers moderating each others' assessment, but this was difficult even among teachers in the same school when priorities were directing attention and resources elsewhere. Thus teachers were working individually and using standard exemplar materials to guide their decisions.

Hall and Harding (2002) reported contrasting approaches to moderation among the six primary schools in their study. In some schools, time was allocated for teachers to meet and to work as a whole school in developing more accurate methods of assessing children. In these schools there was, for example, recognition of the use of portfolios to communicate among teachers, with students and with parents about how work was assessed. In other schools, a decline in the level of collaboration was noted following the initial period in which time had been made available to discuss assessment. Hall and Harding (2002) also noted that schools remained isolated from each other and also largely from the local authority assessment advisers. The advisers potentially had a key role in moderating teachers' assessment and forming a pathway through which teachers could share their understanding of assessment criteria and how to apply them to students' work. They had developed considerable knowledge and expertise in assessment by teachers but found limited opportunities to share this with teachers. A resource which could have been used for moderation was left unused.

Schools need to develop routines which make provision for assessment meetings within and across schools. The value of these practices goes beyond reliable assessment (as discussed later) since 'the quality of teaching and learning inside the classroom is strongly influenced by the quality of professional relationships teachers have with their colleagues outside the classroom' (Hall and Harding, 2002: 12).

Summary of Conditions Affecting Dependability

Before turning to other ways of improving reliability and addressing random inaccuracies as well as systematic bias in teachers' judgments, we will look briefly at the research findings bearing on the conditions that affect the reliability and validity of teachers' summative assessment judgments. Since reliability and validity are interdependent (see Chapter 1) it makes sense to consider them together using the concept of dependability. The main points are

- To increase reliability, there is tension between closer specification of the task and of the conditions under which it is carried out, and the closer specification of the criteria for judging performance.
- Detailed criteria describing levels of progress in various aspects of achievement enable teachers to assess students reliably on the basis of regular classroom work.
- It is important for teachers to follow agreed procedures if teachers' assessment is to be sufficiently dependable to serve summative purposes.
- The training for teachers to improve the reliability of their assessment is more effective when it involves teachers as far as possible in the process of identifying criteria so as to develop ownership of them and understanding of the language used.
- Training should also focus on the sources of potential bias that have been revealed by research.

- Dependable assessment needs protected time for teachers to meet and to take advantage of the support that others, including assessment advisers, can give.
- Moderation through professional collaboration is of benefit to teaching and learning as well as to assessment.

Enhancing Quality of Teachers' Assessment

If a system based on teachers' assessments and extending beyond a single school is to achieve acceptable levels of consistency in the ways that judgments are made then it needs effective quality management procedures. These will include moderation of the procedures that are in place to prevent error and bias (quality assurance) and moderation of the outcomes of assessment to detect any inconsistency in the way that criteria have been applied (quality control). The way in which moderation for these purposes is conducted should be decided with a view to 'quality enhancement', a concept that recognizes the interrelationships of assessment with the curriculum and with pedagogy. Quality enhancement refers to the wider benefit of schemes for quality assurance and quality control, going beyond the dependability of assessment results to affect the quality of students' learning opportunities. The following discussion draws on some material in Harlen (1994).

Quality Control

Quality control refers to the adjustment of the outcomes of an assessment once it has been made; it therefore takes place after the event. It is particularly used in relation to the results of examinations that lead to an award. The main options available for ensuring quality dependable outcomes of assessment are described in the following.

Statistical moderation

This approach involves students taking a test which is externally marked, is often quite short and assesses general ability rather than the specific learning being assessed by the teachers' judgment. It is particularly useful in cases where it is known that teachers can rank order students with considerable accuracy (as happens in modern foreign languages, for instance) but where there is variation in levels from one teacher to another. Use of the test identifies any differences between groups or classes assessed by different teachers and results in all the scores of one group being moved up or down but the rank order of students within the group staying the same. It is also used in attempts to equalize results in different subjects or domains of differing difficulty, in which cases the rank order of students may be changed. The process is out of the hands of the teacher once the assessment and tests have been completed.

Inspection of samples at a distance or by a visiting moderator
In this approach, the teachers' judgments of work for an external award are checked by the awarding body. A sample of students' work is examined in relation to how it was set, marked and graded. According to circumstances, this may be through a visit to the school or college or by means of samples sent from the school. In either case the awarding body sets out how the sample should be selected so that the teacher does not exercise choice in this matter. The main difference between moderation at a distance and by a visiting moderator or verifier is that, in the latter case, there can be professional discussion with the school or college staff about the process as well as the products of the assessment.

External examiners (higher education)
This involves staff from one institution visiting another institution in order to establish some comparability of standards across higher education institutions where assessment, both by examinations and coursework, is controlled entirely within each institution. It usually involves both visits and studying samples at a distance.

Appeals
In the case of external examinations, re-marking or review of the examination process can be initiated by the teacher if the results for a student, or group of students, are out of line with expectations. In the case of teachers' assessment it is the student who would initiate the re-assessment of their work.

Group moderation
Here there is routine review, at a meeting of teachers, of samples of students' work which have been assessed by their teachers. For assessment for external purposes the group should comprise teachers from different schools.

Quality Assurance

Quality assurance procedures concern the process of arriving at results and aim to ensure that this is done in a way that is fair and unbiased. This usually takes place before any judgments are made but in some circumstances can operate after the event, in which case the procedures resemble those for quality control, suggesting that there is no sharp distinction between these two functions. The five main alternatives are as follows.

Defining criteria

As the research cited earlier on page 72 indicated, when teachers rate the extent to which certain goals of learning have been achieved without the guidance of criteria for what is meant by 'good' or 'poor' achievement, the reliability of the results is low. Criteria are needed, indicating what aspects of the work are significant and on what basis they are to be judged. Criteria can be stated at different levels of detail and can be task-specific or more general. One of the main dilemmas of criterion-referenced assessment is deciding among these alternatives. The more detailed the statements, the more numerous they are and, in the extreme, they become unable to reflect complex and particularly higher-level learning outcomes. On the other hand, more general statements can be more ambiguous and less easy to use reliably. Both research (Rowe and Hill, 1996; Frederiksen and White, 2004; Hargreaves et al., 1996; Shavelson et al., 1992) and practice (see Chapter 7) suggest that criteria that describe a development in understanding or skills, but are not task specific, provide the best help for reliable assessment by teachers.

Exemplification

Providing examples of work and showing how certain aspects relate to the criteria of assessment help in conveying what the criteria mean in practice. Good examples also indicate the opportunities that students need in order to show their achievement of skills or understanding. Thus although the outcome of assessment is identified, the focus is on the process of arriving at that outcome. Examples can be used in group moderation, but are particularly useful for individual teachers unable to participate in a group moderation meeting.

Accreditation

In this approach to quality assurance, the body responsible for an external award approves a school or an individual teacher as able to conduct assessment according to set standards. This has been practice for some time in the award of vocational qualifications, where responsibility for assessment is devolved to centres (schools, colleges or work-places) and trained assessors and 'internal' verifiers ensure that procedures have been followed. There is some sampling of portfolios where relevant. The awarding bodies regularly send 'external' verifiers to visit centres and report on the assessment procedures, taking action if necessary to ensure comparability across centres.

A more recent move is that proposed by the SHA (the Secondary Heads Association, now the Association of School and College Leaders) for awarding bodies to give certain experienced teachers the status of 'chartered examiner' (ASCL, 2006). The proposal is that chartered examiners carry out, or oversee, internal assessment that is part of an external award. Generally, a large school would have several chartered examiners in each subject, and a senior chartered assessor with overall responsibility for standards. An alternative proposal, made in the Daugherty Review of the school curriculum and assessment in Wales (ACCAC, 2004), is for schools to be accredited in conducting assessment by teachers in accord with the requirements of statutory assessment and reporting. Procedures would be monitored by external verifiers, whilst the outcomes of assessing a sample of student portfolios would be checked by external moderators.

Visits by verifiers or moderators

Whether or not schools or teachers are accredited, this approach provides quality assurance of teachers' assessment by visits to review procedures. Verifiers discuss and, in some cases, observe how assessment is carried out. The focus is on evidence being gathered and the criteria used and so the visit can take place at any time, as distinct from visits for the purpose of ensuring fair outcomes once judgments have been made. The intention is to influence the process of assessment and in this way ensure greater reliability of the results for all students.

Group moderation

This involves teachers meeting to review samples of students' work, much as for quality control, but the discussion is wider ranging and aimed at ensuring shared understandings of criteria and how they are applied. In practice both quality assurance and quality control purposes are generally combined with a professional development function, depending on the discussion going beyond the agreement on grades or levels for particular students. It is useful for such meetings to involve a local authority moderator or adviser, who is able to note the training needs of teachers.

Comparing Quality Procedures

From a discussion of various systems for assessment, Harlen (1994) provides an evaluation of these procedures in terms of six aspects: the extent to which the moderation procedures are bureaucratically controlled; their contribution to professional development; their demand in terms of time; their cost; and their impact on the process and on the product of assessment. The judgments were summarized by giving a rough rating from one (low) to three (high) for each aspect, producing the profiles given in Table 5.1.

Looking down the columns gives a rough idea of how approaches compare for each aspect. As might be expected, those approaches mainly concerned with quality control have the greatest impact on the product, or outcome, of the assessment, but it is argued that those concerned with quality assurance also impact on the product, perhaps not directly but indirectly through improvement of the procedures. If we consider how each

Table 5.1 Profiles of moderation procedures

Approach	Bureaucratic	PD value	Time	Cost	Impact on process	Impact on product
Statistical	***	–	*	*	–	***
Inspection of samples	*	*	*	*	–	**
External examining	*	*	**	***	*	**
Group moderation of grades	*	**	**	***	**	**
Defining criteria	–	**	**	*	*	**
Exemplification	–	**	*	*	**	**
Accreditation	–	**	*	*	***	**
Verifier visits	–	**	***	***	***	*
Group moderation of process	–	***	***	***	***	**

(Adapted from Harlen, 1994: 140)

contributes to quality enhancement, which embraces the impact on both product and process, and the wider contribution to teaching and learning of professional development, then group moderation is identified as being the prime approach closely followed by moderator visits and accreditation.

At present not enough is known about the possible impact of accrediting schools or teachers beyond the context of vocational education, but many schools have appointed assessment co-ordinators and taken responsibility for improving the quality of internal assessment. For confidence that standards are consistent across schools, however, some element of external control is needed. The means of doing this should be decided in the context of quality enhancement, which points to moderation procedures that support teacher professional development. 'To do otherwise sets up a self-fulfilling prophecy which lowers teachers' professional status and so reduces public confidence in their judgements' (Harlen, 1994: 145).

Finally, it is part of the remit of the Institute of Educational Assessors (IEA) established in 2006 to contribute to the quality enhancement of assessment by teachers as well as to the expertise of those involved in tests and examinations. The IEA is an independent professional body 'committed to improving the quality of assessment by working with others to offer professional support and development ... thereby sustaining and increasing public confidence in assessment standards' (IEA, 2006).

6 Summative assessment by teachers in action: examples in England

In this chapter the four required properties of assessment introduced in Chapter 1 are used to consider the assessment procedures used at three different points in the system in England: the Foundation Stage Profile (FSP), the end-of-Key Stage teachers' assessment at Key Stages 1 to 4 and the National Vocational Qualifications.

In the FSP, teachers assess children between the ages of 3 and 5 in terms of nine points of development on 13 scales. Several staff take part in creating the record, which is built up gradually, and in moderating final judgments. Thus the validity and reliability of the record are potentially high. The main threats are that the coverage of the curriculum may not be as wide as intended and that the sheer number of decisions to be made induces a mechanistic approach that can undermine validity.

The procedures for the end-of-Key-Stage judgments don't include records being built up as in the FSP but instead involve teachers relating evidence from a range of activities to the more general criteria of the 'level' descriptions. In the primary school, teachers use a variety of methods as well as the recommended 'best fit' approach. At KS3 there is a greater tendency to use special tasks incorporated into classroom work as a source of evidence. Teacher-assessed coursework in end-of-Key-Stage 4 (GCSE) assessment is potentially more valid than examinations for certain learning outcomes, but becomes more standardized and of lower validity under the pressure of high stakes.

In the third example the criteria for the assessment of NVQs are spelled out in considerable detail, identifying what is required at each competence level in a particular occupation. As in the other examples, learning activities provide evidence for the assessment, but there is a far closer relationship between the training and the competence criteria than in the case of school assessment. Whilst this is intended to ensure high validity, it can also have the opposite effect through fragmenting learning.

Introduction

The examples of summative assessment by teachers described in this chapter span the course of compulsory schooling, from Foundation Stage to age 16 and vocational education beyond school. The system context affects how assessment is practised and these examples, all coming from England, combine to spell out that context. Examples from countries outside England are given in Chapter 7.

It becomes clear from the examples here that, apart from at the Foundation Stage, the system of assessment in England puts pressure in one way or another on teachers through the use of assessment results for evaluation of the effectiveness of teachers, schools and local authorities. The experience of students between the ages of 5 and 16 is of test-dominated assessment. Despite the official requirement for most subjects being the reporting of teachers' assessments, the 'testing ethos' induced by high stakes use of test results leads to widespread use of non-statutory tests and teacher-made tests. It is useful, then, that the examples of the Foundation Stage Profile and National Vocational Qualifications show that alternatives to tests and examinations can operate effectively.

In each example, there is an outline of the assessment content, processes and regulations. This is followed by a summary of how the teachers' assessment element meets the four criteria introduced in Chapter 1. The material in this chapter draws in part on papers written by experts in assessment at the stages described, presented and discussed at seminars of the Assessment Systems for the Future project in 2004 and 2005. The full sources can be accessed from the ARG website as indicated in the footnotes.

The Foundation Stage Profile in England[1]

The Foundation Stage was formally introduced in 2000 as a statutory stage in the National Curriculum in England. It begins when a child is 3 years old, if he or she is receiving government-funded nursery education, or at a later stage when the child begins nursery or primary education. It finishes at the end of the reception year. (Year 1 of primary school begins in the September following a child's fifth birthday.) Soon after the introduction of the Foundation Stage curriculum, a Profile was introduced as 'a way of summarizing young children's achievements at the end of the foundation stage' (QCA, 2003:1). This account focuses on the design and intended procedures of the Profile, pending a full evaluation of its use and impact in practice.

[1] This section draws on material written by Paul Newton in a paper prepared for ASF Seminar 2 and by David Bartlett in ASF Working Paper 4. Both available on the ASF section of the ARG website at www.assessment-reform-group.org.

Children are likely to attend different types of setting during the Foundation Stage, for example, beginning at a pre-school playgroup and ending up in a school's reception class. Most children will have joined a reception class during the last year of the Foundation Stage. The curriculum for the Foundation Stage is identified within six areas of learning:

- personal, social and emotional development;
- communication, language and literacy;
- mathematical development;
- knowledge and understanding of the world;
- physical development;
- creative development.

For each of these areas, there are early learning goals that define the expected achievements at the end of the Foundation Stage. For each early learning goal, a series of 'stepping stones' highlights expected progress. Assessment is based entirely upon the professional judgment of practitioners; there are no formal tests or tasks. Staff (practitioners) are expected to assess children's progress throughout the foundation stage to establish appropriate next steps in learning for planning purposes. Assessment of attainment at the end of the Foundation Stage is statutory and must be carried out according to the Foundation Stage Profile.

The Foundation Stage Profile (FSP) was introduced as a statutory requirement in 2002–3 and was designed to reflect a new approach to assessment, since it was to be built up by the practitioner without the use of tests or tasks. It reflects the recognition that during the early years children typically do not produce 'work' which can be easily marked. There is also no systematic collection of a portfolio of 'evidence'.

The FSP is intended to support both assessment for learning (formative assessment) and assessment of learning (summative assessment). It comprises 13 scales within the six areas of learning and nine points within each scale, where:

- points 1 to 3 describe a child who is still progressing towards the achievements set out in the early learning goals, and are based mainly on the stepping stones;
- points 4 to 8 describe a child who is making progress in achieving the early learning goal;
- point 9 describes a child who has achieved all of points 1 to 8 and who is working consistently beyond the level of the early learning goals.

For recording purposes, an optional 'scale booklet' enables practitioners to record progress for each child during the reception year. For each of the 13 scales, the scale booklet presents a box for each of the nine points, within which there is a performance description. Below each box are three dots for recording where children have reached in each of the three terms during the year. There is also space for a small number of comments. However, practitioners may use other forms of recording as long as these are based on the early learning goals.

The three bands are hierarchical and this is also the case for points 1 to 3 within the first band of each scale. However, points 4 to 8 are ordered according to the percentage of children achieving them in trials during the development of the FSP. Children may be assigned a later point without necessarily having been assigned an earlier one. It is intended that the judgment should be based upon information from all those adults who interact with the child in that setting, as well as upon information from practitioners in previous settings and from parents. It is therefore intended to represent evidence of attainment, even when that evidence may not have been demonstrated within a formal educational context.

There is a *FSP Handbook* (QCA, 2003) that provides information and advice on using the scales, case studies and exemplification, and gives guidance on moderation and use with children having special needs or English as an additional language. This provides help for practitioners in judging a child's typical attainment at a particular time, through a process of 'best fit' between the child's behaviour and the performance description/exemplification materials.

The FSP is based on the assumption that practitioners build up evidence for their assessments throughout the Reception Year on a cumulative basis, from on-going teaching and learning, and that they will be able to make most judgments for each scale on the basis of this evidence. Occasionally, additional observations (of behaviour in different contexts) may be required, although these should still be situated within the normal curriculum provision.

Properties of the Foundation Stage Assessment

Validity

The construct validity of the FSP is potentially high, given that it covers all of the areas of learning for the Foundation Stage and includes all of the early learning goals. Judgments are made as to whether children have achieved particular early learning goals using a wide evidence base from on-going learning and teaching, over time and over a range of contexts and learning experiences. However, the curriculum guidance for the Foundation Stage emphasises that learning should be predominantly child-initiated and play-based.

The degree to which the assessments made by practitioners (both teachers and teaching assistants) dependably reflect children's achievements of the early learning goals will depend not only on the coverage of curriculum content, but also on the effective implementation of the intended pedagogy, through child-initiated activities. Thus the high potential validity of the assessment may not be realised until the intended curriculum, itself new to some practitioners, is fully embedded.

Reliability

A characteristic of the FSP is that all practitioners in a setting (teachers, assistants and support staff) should be involved in the assessment of children and in making shared judgments. This suggests a context for moderation among practitioners through which consistency within a setting can be developed. In relation to consistency across settings, the *FSP Handbook* (QCA, 2003) contains a model for moderation within a local education authority, involving both visits to schools and other settings where the FSP is in use and also cluster meetings of schools.

The model provides guidance about the form that visits and cluster meetings could take, although it does not specify these in detail or provide materials to be used. Since the assessment of the points reached by children can only be understood in relation to the contexts within which the judgments are made, moderation meetings also provide a vehicle for practitioners to share information on the ways in which they are implementing the curriculum. Moderation processes are therefore not only a way of developing reliability, but also a powerful vehicle for professional development through the sharing of practice.

Impact

The FSP is intended as a summary of children's achievements by the time they reach the end of the Foundation Stage. Thus its purposes include reporting to parents, to the children's next teachers and to the local authority. However, it also serves other purposes. If judgments for the FSP are made gradually in the way intended, it provides information about children's progress that can be used to inform planning and adjust on-going teaching, prompting practitioners to develop the ways in which they are covering the curriculum. It also promotes a summative assessment model where judgments draw upon the rich assessment evidence arising from on-going learning and teaching. This evidence can be used formatively to help learning in particular situations and then can be summarized against the performance descriptions for the scales for the judgments each term. Successive summative assessments cumulatively produce the end of the Foundation Stage Profile. If the record is not built in this way but completed at the end of the year, its potential for formative use of the evidence is lost. However, completing the judgments at the three recording stages does not in itself ensure that the information has been used formatively. (See Chapter 8 for discussion of the relationship between formative and summative assessment.)

Profile assessments cannot be used to make comparisons between schools in the same way as national test and examination results are used in England, since only aggregated results are submitted to the DfES by local authorities and results for specific schools cannot be identified. Nevertheless, local authorities are still able to produce comparative information for schools and the results from individual schools or settings can be compared with national data at the time of inspections. There are also indications that DfES policy on collecting individual pupil and school data may change in 2007. Accountability judgments are therefore possible and these could have negative consequences for the FSP assessment processes. However, this will depend on how the information is used and the extent to which schools can use it for self-evaluation, rather than seeing themselves as responding to external judgments.

A further consideration in relation to the consequences of the assessment concerns the extent to which the results are used for another key purpose, to inform Year 1 teachers. There have been difficulties here since the FSP reflects achievement of the early learning goals rather than being expressed in terms of the National Curriculum attainment targets that Year 1 teachers are familiar with. In addition, the child-initiated learning of the Foundation Stage contrasts with the relatively more formal approach that can characterize teaching and learning in Key Stage 1. The combination of these two factors may have resulted in some Year 1 teachers making little use of the FSP information and attributing little validity to the assessments that they receive. However, both local and national initiatives are being implemented to address these transition issues, with teachers developing their understanding and use of FSP assessments and the Foundation Stage approach to learning.

Resources

If the FSP is not built gradually in the way intended, practitioners are faced with the unmanageable and time-consuming task of summarizing all of their judgments towards the end of the Reception Year for all of the children in a class. While this may serve the purposes of reporting to parents and the next teacher and provide the required information for external data collection, it would clearly be an exercise of limited usefulness. If the FSP is built up gradually over time, manageability is in the hands of practitioners. It does not require the collection of any evidence to support judgments over and above that normally available from on-going learning and teaching, although practitioners need to have a good knowledge of the curriculum and be able to articulate the judgments they are making.

The scope of any system utilising teacher assessment is potentially problematic because over time large amounts of information can be generated that can be difficult to summarize and interpret if records are paper-based.

The electronic record for the FSP (the eProfile) is a solution to this, in that it summarizes assessments in a way that makes them manageable and accessible so that they can be used to inform planning for classes, groups and individual children. While its use is not a requirement, without it practitioners can experience manageability problems and much of the power of the FSP for monitoring and planning can be undermined.

Three circumstances have affected the quality of the implementation of the FSP. First, it was introduced in a hurried way part way through the 2002–03 school year with practitioners expected to summarize their first assessments by the end of that school year. This did not allow them time to familiarize themselves with the FSP, made it difficult for local authorities to organize the first round of training, and in any case was inappropriate given that it was designed to be built up gradually over successive years. Further, as can be inferred from the description of the recording process for each child, the number of judgments to be made was seen by many teachers as imposing an unduly burdensome requirement on reception year staff. Combined with the slow implementation of training, this created a situation in which teachers followed the requirements rather mechanically, missing the potential benefits.

The second point concerns the variation in support across the country for the development of moderation procedures. In some local authorities moderation was soon well developed and in addition, in some parts of the country, there are annual regional conferences for moderators to develop consistent approaches and interpretation of the FSP scales. In other areas moderation processes were developed only when, in the third full year of the FSP, support was provided by the National Assessment Agency (NAA).

The third point concerns continuity within the curriculum and the assessment of the system as a whole. As noted earlier, Year 1 teachers receiving the information were unfamiliar with the formulation of the early years curriculum and its goals. Clearly, where changes are made to the summative assessment processes for any part of an education system, it is essential that the potential impact on other parts of a system be given proper consideration.

End of Key Stage Assessment by Teachers in England[2]

The National Curriculum in England, phased in from 1990, established a uniform curriculum and assessment described within these four stages of the compulsory education:

2 This section draws upon some of the material written by Paul Newton in a paper prepared for ASF Seminar 2, available on the ARG website at http://k1.ioe.ac.uk/tlrp/arg/ASF-report2.htm#F and by Gordon Stobart in ASF Working Paper 4 http://k1.ioe.ac.uk/tlrp/arg/ASF-workingpaper4.htm

- Key Stage 1 (Years 1 and 2)
- Key Stage 2 (Years 3 to 6)
- Key Stage 3 (Years 7 to 9)
- Key Stage 4 (Years 10 and 11)

There are 12 National Curriculum subjects, five of which are statutory at all four key stages, and the first three being identified as 'core' subjects:

1 English
2 mathematics
3 science
4 information and communication technology
5 physical education.

The remaining seven subjects are only statutory at certain Key Stages:

6 history (1 to 3)
7 geography (1 to 3)
8 design and technology (1 to 3)
9 art and design (1 to 3)
10 music (1 to 3)
11 modern foreign languages (3)
12 citizenship (3 and 4).

Although separate programmes of study exist at each Key Stage, specifying the subject matter, skills and processes that should be taught during the Key Stage, the National Curriculum is built on an assumption of progress across key stages. This progression is expressed in terms of eight levels of attainment plus a level of exceptional performance above Level 8. Each level spans roughly two years and students are judged to have attained, or been awarded, a 'level' when their performance meets the criteria expressed in the level descriptions – short paragraphs indicating typical performance at each level.

Key Stages 1 to 3

For the core subjects of English, mathematics and science, there are external tests and tasks which schools are required to administer in a strictly-controlled manner at the end of Key Stages 1 (English and mathematics), 2 and 3. At the end of Key Stage 4 assessment is in the form of the GCSE examination. In addition to the core subject tests at the end of Key Stages 1 to 3, assessment by teachers is also required. For Key Stages 2 and 3 both test results and teachers' assessment results are reported and are said to have equal status. From 2005, at Key Stage 1 only the teachers' assessment results are reported but tests in English and mathematics still have to be given to inform the teachers' judgments. Schools are required to provide end-of-Key-Stage judgments based on teachers' judgments for other, non-core, subjects at Key Stage 3.

Whilst it is only at the end of a Key Stage that students' performance must be reported in terms of National Curriculum levels, schools have a statutory requirement to provide a summative report for parents for each student and each subject studied at least once a year. Schools often choose to include the levels judged to have been reached. This trend towards annual reporting in terms of levels has been reinforced by widespread use of the optional tests produced by QCA for the years between the ends of key stages for the core subjects.

How teachers conduct summative assessment to reach their judgments is not part of the legislation, but there is a requirement that the process is one of finding the 'best fit' with the level descriptions. This means considering a range of performance for each student and comparing it with the description of the most likely level, and with descriptions for the adjacent levels, to decide the best match. In practice, as reported by Gipps and Clarke (1998) teachers used a variety of strategies, often more intuitive than analytical. There is also guidance on moderation procedures to support consistency in teachers' judgments, but moderation is not a requirement.

As mentioned in Chapter 4, at Key Stage 3 there appears to be little time given to moderation meetings and teachers depend on internal or end-of-module tests as well as on classwork. There is a growing practice of teachers at Key Stage 3 using specially-designed tasks for their teachers' assessment, either devised externally (as in *Monitoring Pupils' Progress in English at Key Stage 3* (QCA, 2006a)) or created by groups of teachers. These tasks are designed on the basis of the National Curriculum level descriptions, thus ensuring a match between the evidence and the criteria that simplifies the process of judgment and improves reliability.

In January 2007 the DfES published, for consultation, proposals for tests at each level which may eventually replace end-of-key-stage tests (DfES, 2007). The 'tests for progress' would be taken by pupils when teachers' assessment indicates their readiness for a test at a particular level. The aim is to provide information about progress more frequently than at the end of key stages, using externally marked tests in English and mathematics at each level. Although the proposals claim to facilitate the use of assessment for learning, they do not address some of the concerns discussed here about factors that inhibit this formative use. For example, they reinforce the use of levels attained by pupils as the basis of targets for school evaluation, which can mean that whatever the basis of the assessment it has the disadvantages associated with high stakes. Moreover, there is no mention of the professional development necessary for teachers to improve their use of assessment data for both formative and summative purposes.

Key Stage 4

Assessment at the end of Key Stage 4 is essentially external; students are usually following courses that lead to the award of formal qualifications provided by national awarding bodies. These qualifications include the General Certificate of Secondary Education (GCSE) and National Vocational Qualification (NVQ). NVQ courses are assessed by teachers or vocational trainers through work-place activities and portfolios of evidence; these are discussed in the next section. Here we focus on GCSE assessment.

Within the GCSE there is both internal and external assessment. Internal assessment generally has a lower weighting than external assessment, although there tends to be a greater emphasis upon internal assessment within certain creative and practical subjects. The internally-assessed element is intended to cover those aspects of the subject not easily assessed through written examinations. A typical GCSE assessment involves the student taking two examinations, which are externally marked, and submitting coursework which is teacher assessed and externally moderated. The examinations generally account for around 75 per cent of the final mark (less in more applied subjects) with the coursework contributing the rest. Coursework ranges from specific practical activities to written assignments or portfolios. In order to increase reliability, many coursework tasks are designed by the awarding body and are completed by students in the classroom within a specified time period.

Properties of End-of-Key-Stage Assessment by Teachers

Validity

The approach to assessment by teachers at the end of Key Stages 1, 2 and 3 is considerably less systematic than in the case of the Foundation Stage. This means that the evidence used may not reflect the full range of the curriculum and what is taken into account will vary from one teacher to another. The tendency for teachers to follow, in their own assessment, the pattern of the external tests may further reduce what is assessed to what is readily tested. Both the problematic quality of teacher-made tests and the uncertain relevance of commercial tests to the particular experiences of students throw doubt on the validity of teachers' judgments based on test results. Thus in practice the validity of teachers' judgments might be lower than it would be in theory if more systematic procedures for gathering and interpreting evidence from a range of classroom activities and for moderating judgments were in place.

In GCSE at the end of Key Stage 4, the coursework element offers, in principle, an opportunity for a fuller sampling of the domain and the subject skills involved. However, successive moves to contain and standardize this element have meant that in practice, especially in mathematics and science, it has often been little more than a prescribed classroom exercise which has limited validity and fitness-for-purpose. Further concerns about the possibility of plagiarism, particularly from use of the internet (where some 'model answers' can be found) and help from parents – and in some cases from teachers who provide highly structured templates – were revealed in a review of coursework conducted by the QCA (2005) and also in a review of teachers' views on coursework carried out for the QCA by Mori (QCA, 2006b). Concerns about coursework culminated in the announcement of new arrangements relating to it to be implemented in 2009 (QCA, 2006c). As a result, in some subjects coursework set by teachers will be discontinued and replaced by controlled assessments, whilst in other subjects, particularly those having a practical element, internal assessment will continue with greater safeguards being introduced.

Reliability

As with validity, the accuracy of teachers' judgments in end-of-Key-Stages 1, 2 and 3 assessment could potentially be higher than national tests, since they can use far more evidence than can be encompassed within a short test. This avoids the errors introduced in tests by having to use evidence from only a sample of possible work.

However, as we have noted in Chapter 5, evidence from research suggests that conditions for high reliability include the existence and systematic use of general criteria, training to reduce sources of bias and error and moderation procedures. In the absence of these conditions any measures of the reliability of teachers' assessment in National Curriculum assessment are likely to underestimate what can be achieved. Further, as noted in Chapter 5, estimates based on correlations between teachers' assessment and test results are of questionable value, given that the test results are of low accuracy (Chapter 4). Consequently the reliability of teachers' judgments in National Curriculum assessment is unknown.

For external awards at the end of Key Stage 4 there is a Code of Practice which applies to GCSE, specifying what awarding bodies need to do to ensure standardization of marking and moderation of internal assessment. Instructions, supported by training when changes are introduced, are provided for teachers in task-setting, marking and internal moderation. Assessment criteria for coursework are published by awarding bodies. For quality control, once internal assessments have been made, the Code of Practice requires awarding bodies to moderate marks submitted. For example, a sample of written coursework from several centres is reviewed and, if necessary, marks are adjusted for all the candidates from a centre, keeping the rank order of students the same. The changes to coursework arrangements mentioned above will require some modification of these procedures.

Impact

Although it would seem that assessment by teachers plays a major role in the National Curriculum assessment, since the national tests are confined to the core subjects at the end of the Key Stages, in practice the high stakes attached to tests mean that testing dominates the whole process, with teachers making widespread use of non-statutory and commercial tests. Results for tests in English, mathematics and science (for Key Stages 2, 3 and 4) are published in national performance tables. Corresponding results for teachers' assessment are not published in these tables, although they may be published separately by LEAs (Local Education Authorities). Schools are required to publish aggregate results, from all statutory end-of-Key-Stage assessments (both test and teacher assessment results) in school prospectuses and governors' annual reports. Schools are also required to transfer statutory assessment results for individual students to new schools when students move. Results for non-core subjects are used by external bodies such as LEAs, OfSTED inspectors and the DfES, creating a pressure, perceived or real, for 'hard evidence' that leads to a good deal of use of internal testing using teacher-made or commercial tests (James, 2000; Harlen, 2006c). Consequently, there is much less use of evidence from regular work than there is, for instance, in the FSP, and less opportunity to use assessment formatively as well as summatively.

Any impact of teachers' assessment is thus overshadowed by the high stakes attached to national tests. This results in the previously discussed narrow focusing on those subjects and aspects of subjects that are tested and the drilling of students in strategies that enable them to pass tests, even if they do not have the underlying skills and knowledge.

GCSE results have high stakes for students as they may influence further progression in education, as well as high stakes for teachers and schools since the proportion of students reaching grade C is used as a key indicator of a school's performance and the basis for creating national league tables. Although coursework provides only a small proportion of the marks in most subjects, and is set to reduce further in 2009, the high stakes pressure leads to closer control of coursework and the conditions in which it is carried out, with a consequent threat to validity.

Resources

Assessment by teachers, as originally conceived in the report of the Task Group on Assessment and Testing (DES/WO, 1988), made considerable demands on teachers partly due to the over-prescribed nature of the first drafts of the National Curriculum. Following a review of the curriculum the process of assessment by teachers was simplified, so that teachers were required to make a smaller number of holistic judgments for each student at the end of the school year. Some supporting materials were also produced and a range of methods for moderating teachers' judgments was also recommended, but schools were not required to use the materials or follow the advice. With tests dominating, the time spent on teachers' assessment was minimized in most schools at the expense of the quality of the judgments and the use of assessment for formative purposes.

The standardization and moderation procedures required for assessing coursework in GCSE examinations clearly take teachers' time and account for a proportion of the entrance fee paid to awarding bodies. However, this time and cost pale into insignificance in comparison with the resources of time and money needed to sustain external examinations. Transporting millions of scripts to schools, from schools to markers, and back to the examination body, is only the externally visible part of the resources required. Within schools, the written examinations take up days of potential learning and teaching time through preparation, mock examinations, organizing and invigilating, as well as the disruption to the whole school when examinations are taking place. Greater use of coursework would require greater time for moderation meetings, but these have benefits beyond the reliability of the assessment results. Many of the problems of coursework as currently practised could be overcome by assessing 'the work of the course' rather than specific pieces of coursework.

National Vocational Qualifications in England[3]

National Vocational Qualifications (NVQs) were introduced in 1989, in a radical and controversial overhaul of work-based qualifications. The aim was to update and improve the quality of work-place training by reflecting the demands of employers for key competences in specific occupational roles. NVQs can be taken whilst working in a job or apprenticeship scheme, on a specific course in a college, on a qualification and training programme offered by a training provider, or a mixture of these provisions. In these contexts an assessor in the college or work place gathers evidence in relation to detailed specifications of competence in different roles, the range of contexts in which competence must be demonstrated and the indicators of performance that show it has been achieved.

The specifications of competence and criteria for assessing and accredit-

3 This section draws upon material written by Kathryn Ecclestone in ASF Working Paper 4, available on the ARG website at http://k1.ioe.ac.uk/tlrp/arg/ASF-workingpaper4.htm

ing them were created initially by industry lead bodies representing employers' interests in different occupational sectors. These bodies were reorganized as sector skills councils in the 2001 Learning and Skills Act. Sector skills councils are responsible for creating and updating the specifications to reflect employers' needs in different organizations within a particular sector, such as retail. An NVQ comprises units of competence that can be taken and accredited separately or as part of a whole qualification. They were designed to be available from entry level to employment up to degree level and professional equivalents.

Undoubtedly, the system of work-based qualifications that has developed is complex. There are thousands of vocational qualifications, hundreds of awarding bodies and thousands of training providers including FE colleges, employers and private training organizations. In addition to being accredited by long-established, well-known and respected vocational bodies such as City & Guilds, NVQs can be accredited by unions, professional organizations, sector-specific bodies and small awarding bodies.

Assessment demands are centred on what learners (who are often also employees) can do, and can be seen to do, in relation to the tasks required of them for competent practice. Detailed specifications of outcomes and assessment criteria promote and demand 'mastery', that is, success in all requirements, as opposed to compensation and grading in examinations such as the GCSE. Meeting the criteria may be judged from evidence in a variety of forms: observation by supervisors and/or external assessors; written testimony by colleagues or managers; written assignments; practical tasks; oral feedback and testimony. There is a strong emphasis on assessment tasks being 'fit-for-purpose' and the validity of assessment as opposed to reliability. Candidates are assessed 'when ready' but can repeat assessment tasks as often as necessary until they are deemed to be competent, producing assessment decisions of 'not yet competent' or 'competent'. Assessment evidence in relation to the criteria is used formatively until competence is demonstrated. This process can, however, cause a narrow focus on meeting the detailed performance criteria, which may not be the same as developing knowledge and skills related to the required competences. Moreover, the large number of detailed criteria that have to be applied can induce a mechanistic approach in the assessors, particularly when dealing with a number of candidates.

Properties of NVQ Assessment

Validity

The NVQ was designed with validity as its central goal in order to ensure that assessment was fit-for-purpose, was 'employer-led' and based on authentic, real-life tasks for specific occupations. In some cases this authenticity of work-based tasks is compromised by simulation of activities, for example in colleges, and by a lack of access to the full range of occupational tasks needed to make up a unit of competence.

There are also questions about how far the diverse range of methods used as 'evidence of competence' in NVQs reflects the learning being assessed. The extent to which specific tasks and tests, designed both as learning and assessment activities, reflect the full range of skills, attitudes and creative and critical thinking skills is questionable and varies amongst NVQs. A further threat to validity is the reduction of learning to a set of easily-assessed outcomes. This can have the result of fragmenting learning so that broader understandings and skills may be missed. Then the assessment may not fully represent the learning that is intended.

Reliability

Because of the sheer variety of practices, providers and programmes, awarding bodies place more emphasis on verifying that procedures and guidance have been adhered to than on moderating assessment decisions. So, although there is some moderation of a sample of assessment decisions, reliability as a feature of NVQs perhaps takes a different form than in other qualifications. In the context of NVQs, reliability means that the evidence used reflects the occupational standards of competence rather than the consistency of judgments across different centres for the same assessment. (Although this seems more like validity, the validity issue is whether the standards reflect the requirements of the occupation.) Comparability of outcomes and across training providers is arrived at through tight specifications of tasks and procedures.

The chief source of low reliability in NVQs is the local, individual nature of interpretation of evidence by assessors. Institutions are required to carry out internal verification and moderation of procedures and outcomes, with some sampling of portfolios. Awarding bodies follow this up with annual visits to providers by a subject specialist and issue annual reports about the national standards of work in each area.

Impact

The QCA, which oversees the whole awarding system, does not collect national data to compare centres and providers in terms of NVQ outcomes. However, NVQ outcomes are used to judge the institution's or organization's overall achievement rates, and where NVQs are funded by the Learning and Skills Council these outcomes are monitored as part of national targets for the achievement of NVQs at different levels. Teaching and training focus on the summative outcomes, but this is as much a product of the strong criterion-referenced format and the emphasis on teacher/assessor assessment as it is of the way that outcomes are used for accountability. Thus a tendency to focus on a narrow interpretation of criteria and on performance rather than learning is not solely because of excessive accountability for summative results. It is also because of resource pressures to get trainees through the process as cost effectively as possible and a result of the closely specified and prescriptive competences and criteria.

Resources

The running costs of NVQs are high because of the intensity of the assessment process and its individual focus. There is wide variation in quality of training underpinning the assessment process, in terms of time spent on training, individual reviews and portfolio building. Assessors also report spending a great deal of time translating the criteria, tracking the evidence in the portfolios, and generally auditing and managing assessment and quality assurance processes for the awarding bodies in a complex and prescriptive assessment regime.

In addition, where providers offer different NVQs from different awarding bodies, the administrative and quality assurance costs can be very high: a large college, for example, might pay fees to 20 different awarding bodies in order to offer NVQs and other vocational qualifications. This also requires creating links between different quality assurance procedures for verification and moderation. Some public sector organizations such as the Royal Mail and the National Health Service are required to offer NVQs for which the cost is publicly subsidized. This has been a significant factor in establishing and maintaining NVQs.

Comment

All the examples here make a good deal of use of assessment by teachers and offer the opportunity for assessment to be used to help learning as well as to report on learning. However, the Foundation Stage Profile and the Key Stage 1, 2 and 3 assessments also show that it is not enough to provide opportunity for formative use of assessment. What are also required are the training, examples and time to enable it to be a permanent part of the system. Providing these is likely to mean some review of priorities within schools and pre-school settings and the demonstration of its importance through inclusion in the criteria for self-evaluation and evaluation by inspectors.

Also clear from the arrangements for end-of-Key-Stage assessment is that including assessment by teachers does not lead to the dependable and useful results that are needed as long as tests exist and are given high stakes through their use for target-setting and for creating league tables based on the test results. Meanwhile, the NVQ experience indicates that pressures of different kinds can lead to narrow interpretations of criteria, which would need to be avoided if assessment by teachers were the main form of assessment for academic subjects. Moreover, highly specific criteria would not support valid assessment of broad understanding and widely applicable skills, including learning how to learn.

7 Summative assessment by teachers in action: examples in other countries

In this chapter some examples of procedures for using summative assessment by teachers from systems outside England are considered. In the case of Scotland, Wales and Northern Ireland, changes that are in progress or planned for assessment in schools are moving firmly in the direction of greater dependence on assessment by teachers.

The experience of the long-established methods used in the Queensland senior certificate at the end of secondary school are examined and offer some valuable lessons in how to maintain a system based on teachers' judgments that provides results in which all involved have confidence. These lessons include the flexibility to implement the curriculum in a variety of ways, so that the assessment can follow and not determine students' learning experiences. Implications for the nature of the criteria applied are reinforced in the examples of developmental assessment and of the BEAR project.

Other key factors are openness, support for formative use of evidence and moderation of the outcomes. When these are in place the assessment is likely to benefit teaching and learning. It is also significant that in the examples in this chapter the assessment results are used for providing information about individual students and are disconnected from the evaluation of schools. These points are revisited in Chapter 9.

Introduction

This chapter gives some examples of assessment systems where teachers' judgments play a key role from countries outside England. They come from various levels of education including higher education and both low and high stakes assessment. The only rationale for this particular selection is that these were discussed in ASF project seminars where the intention was to learn from the experience of countries where summative assessment by teachers was known to be used. We begin with the three countries of the UK where assessment changes have already happened or are currently in progress. These are followed by two examples from Australia and one from the USA. Some common threads are drawn together at the end.

Scotland, Wales and Northern Ireland

In these three countries, as in England, considerable changes were made in arrangements for the assessment of students in the early 1990s. However, these other parts of the UK are ahead of England in reviewing and making some quite radical changes in the assessment systems that have been in place through most of the 1990s. Scotland, having begun major reforms with a review of assessment in 1999, has gone furthest in the UK in implementing change. It is also the largest of the three countries, with about 2,200 primary, 385 non-selective secondary and 57 independent secondary schools. Transfer from primary to secondary school takes place at the end of year 7 (P7), so there are seven years of primary education and four of secondary education before the statutory school leaving age of 16. Wales is in the process of phasing in change and, as of 2007, in Northern Ireland policy changes are being finalized. However, while these countries are at different stages in implementation of change and differ in the details of the change, they have sufficient in common in the direction of the changes, towards greater use of assessment by teachers and away from frequent testing, to warrant discussing them together.

Scotland

The education system in Scotland has been independent of the Westminster parliament since long before the establishment of the Scottish parliament in 1999. Responsibility for education was officially devolved in 1872 but differences between English and Scottish education began much earlier. Indeed some differences in education across the border have their roots in earlier history, before the union between the Scottish and English parliaments in 1707. Scotland had three universities by the end of the fifteenth century and the National Education Act of 1696 (believed to be the world's first) made provision for a school in every parish. Subsequent establishment of schools, leading to a good rate of literacy in the population in the mid-nineteenth century, reflected the high status of education and respect for the teaching force which remain features of Scottish education.

A related characteristic of Scottish education is the preference for consensus rather than regulation. Neither the curriculum nor its assessment is governed by legislation in Scotland, as is the case in the rest of the UK. In the absence of regulation, factors which ensure implementation of changes include a tradition of conforming with central policy, the value given to providing all students with educational opportunities, and wide consultation on changes. Inevitably, achieving consensus is a slow process and often means that change is evolutionary.

When national assessment was introduced in the early 1990s there was a strong role for professional judgment and the formative use of assessment but, as in other countries of the UK, there was an increasing emphasis on standards, target-setting and accountability in the mid- to late 1990s that distorted the curriculum and moved the focus of assessment to measurement (Hutchinson and Hayward, 2005). As a result, a review of assessment and testing arrangements was begun in 1999 and a major programme of reform in assessment, entitled 'Assessment is for Learning', was introduced in 2003. The overall aim was to 'provide a streamlined and coherent system of assessment to ensure pupils, parents, teachers and other professionals have the feedback they need about pupils' learning and development needs' (SEED, 2005a: 1). The Assessment is for Learning (AifL) progamme sought to

- develop good professional practice and confidence in assessment amongst teachers so that their judgments would be dependable;
- put in place credible quality assurance of teachers' judgments locally and nationally, as part of understanding and sharing standards;
- monitor national attainment in a way that provided accurate information about overall standards and trends and at the same time promoted good classroom practice.

The programme was concerned with the whole system of assessment for the age range 3–14. It recognized that such a comprehensive programme of change would have more chance of succeeding if teachers and other staff felt ownership of the new procedures. Thus new procedures to promote and sustain change were developed collaboratively, with groups of schools working together. To this end ten projects were set up, between them dealing with formative assessment, personal learning plans for students, moderation of teachers' assessment, the development of a bank of tests and tasks for moderation of teachers' judgments and a framework for reporting progress to parents and others. Almost all local authorities (30 out of 32) took part in the development of at least one project and by the end of 2004 over 1,500 schools were involved.

On completion of the development programme, the framework for AifL was expressed in terms of three themes: assessment *for* learning, assessment *as* learning (where students participate in assessment and reflection on their learning) and assessment *of* learning. The AifL programme was formally adopted as policy for the education of students aged 3–14 years by ministers (SEED, 2004) and the action proposed included ensuring the participation of all schools by 2007.

The main features of the programme in action are:

- Formative assessment is in operation both for students and for staff, with particular emphasis on self-assessment, setting own goals and reflecting on learning.
- Teachers use a range of evidence from everyday activities to check on students' progress. There are no key stages in Scotland and students are assessed by their teachers as having reached a level of development (identified in the curriculum guidelines by criteria at six levels, A to F) using evidence from regular activities. Assessment against the level criteria is an on-going process; a student may be judged to have reached a level at any time. When confirmed by moderation, this is recorded and then reported at the appropriate time.
- Quality assurance of teachers' judgments of students' performance is through taking part in collaborative moderation within and across schools to share standards and/or by using National Assessment. A circular (SEED, 2005b) advising on practical implications of the implementation of the programme explained collaborative moderation as involving:

> groups of teachers from different classrooms and schools in gathering examples of children's work in particular aspects of the curriculum, agreeing on the criteria for assessing them, carrying out assessment against the criteria, and agreeing their judgements about the quality of the work. The worked examples can then be shared and used with other groups of professionals to help them understand how they might judge standards in the particular curriculum or subject area. (Circular 02, SEED, 2005b)

- Teachers can also make use of a bank of tests and tasks in English and mathematics to moderate their judgment that a student has reached a certain level. The circular continues:

> Another way for teachers to check their judgements against national standards is for them to use externally devised assessments and tests and compare the results with the results of their own classroom assessments, when they judge that children have reached a particular level ... The bank of assessments available to teachers to confirm children's levels of attainment will be built up gradually and extended from 2005, using assessment materials from the new Scottish Survey of Achievement. (Circular 02, SEED, 2005b)

- For monitoring of national standards there is a separate rolling programme of assessment of a sample of students, now called the Scottish Survey of Achievement. Begun in 1983, as the Assessment of Achievement Programme, it was revised in 2003 to include four subjects – English, mathematics, science and social subjects – each assessed in turn once every four years. Samples of students in years P3, P5, P7 and S2 (8, 10, 12 and 14 years of age) are tested in each survey (SEED, 2005c).

- For evaluation of schools, a school self-evaluation toolkit is being developed to support self-evaluation against quality indicators, which include, but are not confined to, student performance data.

In summary, Assessment is for Learning provides an integrated system whereby

> - teacher-led, quality assured assessment judgments routinely provide information which contributes to school and local authority analysis and benchmarking;
> - external assessments for formal qualifications are used only at the point where a student wants a summative record of the level of achievements for use in the wider education or employment community, on 'exit' from a subject, or school education; and
> - information from national monitoring using external assessment is separated from information about pupils and schools and based on a national sample. (Hutchinson and Hayward, 2005: 243)

Assessment for 14–19 year olds

One of the challenges for Scottish education is to extend the full Assessment is for Learning programme throughout the secondary school. However, in terms of summative assessment, teachers already have a key role in external assessment at Standard Grade (GCSE equivalent) and in National Qualification (NQ) courses. The system of National Qualifications has brought together academic and vocational qualifications into a single unit-based system of NQ courses at Access, Intermediate, Higher and Advanced Higher levels (the latter two replacing existing SCE Higher and Certificate of Sixth Year Studies qualifications).

National Qualification courses consist of a number of specified units that must be credited before a candidate can enter for the external assessment leading to a course award. Centres (schools or colleges) are responsible for carrying out unit assessments and for submitting the results (passed, failed or withdrawn) to the Scottish Qualifications Authority (SQA) so that the candidate can enter for the external examination. Most Standard Grade courses, and many NQ units, have internally-assessed elements. Centres are responsible for submitting to the SQA the results of internal assessment that contribute to the course award, based on specified evidence collected by teachers. The results are subject to sample external moderation, either by visiting moderators or by post.

Wales

Until 2000 the curriculum and assessment in Wales were very similar to those in England, having been established by the Education Reform Act of

1988. The main difference in the curriculum was the inclusion of Welsh as a fourth core subject, whilst English was not compulsory at Key Stage 1 in Welsh-medium schools. Following several reviews of the curriculum the Wales Curriculum 2000 was introduced and the decision was taken to end statutory tests/tasks at Key Stage 1 from 2002.

In 2003, the Qualifications, Curriculum and Assessment Authority for Wales (ACCAC, now within the Department for Education, Lifelong Learning and Skills (DELLS) of the Welsh Assembly Government) set up a review of the school curriculum and assessment arrangements, which published its findings in 2004 (ACCAC, 2004). As a result, ACCAC recommended changes in the curriculum and assessment which were largely accepted by the Minister of Education in the Welsh Assembly Government. These were the main changes in assessment recommended in Key Stages 2 and 3:

- The phasing out of tests at the end of Key Stage 2. Formerly, end-of-Key-Stage 2 assessment involved statutory tests and 'best fit' judgments by teachers. From 2005 the assessment of levels reached by students would be based only on the latter.
- The setting up of a system of moderation in order to ensure an acceptable level of consistency in teachers' judgments. This envisaged that schools would be grouped on the basis of notional secondary school catchment areas, with each primary school linked for the purpose of these moderation procedures to a particular secondary school. Primary and secondary teachers from each group of schools would meet twice in each school year for agreement trials using pupils' work in the subjects being assessed. An 'acceptable level of consistency' in this context is interpreted as being such as to give the secondary schools sufficient confidence in the levels of attainment reported to them for the schools to make use of them as benchmark indicators for subsequent progress. It was also proposed that local authorities be encouraged, but not required, to facilitate cross-catchment and cross-authority moderation arrangements with a view to maximizing the convergence of teachers' judgments on a wider basis.
- The phasing out of tests at the end of Key Stage 3 and the continued reporting of end-of-Key-Stage assessment in all subjects based on teachers' 'best fit' judgments in relation to National Curriculum levels.
- The use of data about students' performance to be only one element used in school self-evaluation.
- The use of data about students' performance to be only one element in the monitoring of overall performance at local authority and national levels.

It was also proposed that secondary schools' procedures for assessment would be 'accredited' in a system of verification and moderation developed by ACCAC/DELLS, and that ACCAC/DELLS would also publish guidance material and procedural advice. The establishment of a programme to develop formative assessment was a further recommendation.

With decisions and implementation of some of these far-reaching changes still (in 2007) pending, it is not yet possible to say that the key moves to extend and support the use of assessment by teachers will meet the declared aims. Although the end-of-key-stage tests have been terminated, it is possible, as noted in Chapter 4, for data based on teachers' judgments to be used in a way that has as equally undesirable consequences as in the case of tests. Whilst it has not been the practice in Wales to publish the performance data of individual primary schools, any change in this could distort the assessment and the curriculum. Moreover, the response of teachers to changes that may seem to make large demands on their time will be critical. It will be important for teachers to develop some sense of ownership in order to work through the initial problems and to see the advantages of the changes in terms of facilitating assessment that supports learning and to be sure of necessary training.

Northern Ireland

Although a smaller country than Wales, Northern Ireland, like Scotland, has a long tradition of a separate education system. The body responsible for the curriculum and assessment has, since 1994, been the Council for Curriculum Examinations and Assessment (CCEA), a non-departmental body reporting to the Department of Education in Northern Ireland. The curriculum is described in terms of Key Stages, but these are different from the Key Stages in England. Children move from pre-school into Year 1 in the year in which they reach the age of 5, not after it, so they are on average younger than Year 1 children in the rest of the UK. Key Stage 1 then spans the first four years and Key Stage 2 the next three, so students move into secondary school at the age of 11 or 12. Secondary education is selective and the selection mechanism, the transfer test known as the 11+ examination, has been a defining feature of Northern Ireland education since 1947. The 11+ has not only dominated the curriculum in Years 6 and 7, but has both sustained and been sustained by the prevailing 'testing culture'.

Several reviews of the curriculum and assessment (Harland et al., 1999a, 1999b, 2001, 2002, 2003) and of the selection system in particular (Johnston and McClune, 2000; Leonard and Davey, 2001; Gardner and Cowan, 2005) highlighted a number of problems with the assessment system. At Key Stage 1 there are no tests and reporting of performance is on the basis of assessment by teachers, but there is no quality assurance of these judgments. At Key Stage 2 there are no national tests as such, but teachers are required to use certain external Assessment Units provided by the CCEA to moderate their assessment at the end of the Key Stage. However, instead of being used to confirm teachers' judgments, these tasks are frequently administered as tests and used to determine the level at which children are working. Moderation of teachers' judgments by the CCEA is not felt to be sufficiently rigorous and teachers do not trust the judgment of other teachers and schools, particularly where there is competition to attract pupils in a shrinking catchment area. Moreover, Key Stage 3 teachers put little faith in the assessment of primary school teachers.

At Key Stage 3 the national tests at the end of Year 10 dominate and teachers' assessment is not moderated. There is a preference among teachers and parents for testing as this is considered to be 'objective' and to involve less work for teachers than using their own assessment. Students, too, like the apparent certainty of tests, as noted in Chapter 3. Yet teachers realise that the testing in core subjects is associated with undue focus upon these subjects and distortion of the curriculum. Furthermore, as at earlier stages, there is little use of assessment to help learning.

Recognition of these problems has led to recommendations for change, including the ending of the 11+ transfer tests. Although this will not alter the need for selection, other changes, such as making assessment by teachers and the formative use of assessment major features in a revised system, should mean that primary school children and their parents are better prepared for making realistic decisions about the appropriate secondary school. In new arrangements being planned, all summative assessment at Key Stages 1, 2 and 3 will be teacher-based and moderated on a three year cycle. Several approaches to quality assurance and quality control of teachers' judgments are being considered, including the accreditation of schools, the moderation of procedures and professional development in assessment techniques and standards for teachers, and the sampling of judgments.

Examples from Australia

The Queensland Senior Certificate

Education in Australia is in the jurisdiction of the individual six states and two territories. Given the size of the country it might be expected that the eight systems would have diverged, with inter-state differences as great as those among states in the USA. However, although a single National Curriculum has been resisted, Cumming and Maxwell suggest that 'in most respects, the commonalities of the state systems outweigh their differences and present a more homogeneous front to the world than might first be perceived' (Cumming and Maxwell, 2004: 90). One of these commonalities is that summative assessment incorporates internal assessment by teachers and this applies at the end of secondary education, where the assessment has high stakes for the students in relation to future education or employment. In the cases of the Australian Capital Territory and Queensland, this assessment at the end of Year 12 is entirely assessed by teachers; in the other states there is some external examination as well. The operation of the system of school-based assessment for the Senior Certificate in Queensland is a well-documented example of how such a system can work. It has been in existence since 1972 when Queensland abolished external examinations.

The reasons for the preference for assessment by teachers exactly mirror the arguments made in earlier chapters: that assessment by teachers is able to include a range of learning outcomes, both academic and vocational, and to support rather than to control the curriculum. Maxwell (2004) argues that

> An important principle of school-based assessment is that the assessment is progressive and continuous. One of the aims ... is to alleviate the peak pressure of a single final examination – the one-shot test on which everything depends. This requires not only that the assessment is tailored to the way in which each subject syllabus is implemented by the school but also that assessment occurs progressively over the whole course of study. In other words, the validity of the assessment is improved by assembling the portfolio from a variety of assessment types and contexts. So too is the reliability improved by having many opportunities for the student to demonstrate their knowledge and capability and by collecting the information on many different occasions. (Maxwell, 2004: 2)

The process is portfolio-based and allows a variation in the content so that syllabuses can be implemented with the flexibility to meet local requirements. The common element is the system of progressive criteria against which each portfolio is judged. There is also a strong system for moderation for those subjects that count towards university entrance, which successfully assures the confidence of all concerned in the outcome of the assessment.

The portfolio is built up over the two years of the course, during which time its content will change not only through addition of new material but through replacing older with more recent evidence. It is only the final evidence that is taken into account, although some will have been collected earlier than other evidence. Thus the final or 'exit' portfolio is made up of assessment tasks that represent the *fullest and latest* information on a student's knowledge and capability.

> *Fullest* information means that assessment information must be available on all mandatory aspects of the syllabus. Important criteria cannot be skipped; the assessment evidence in the portfolio must cover all the required aspects of the course. In some cases, a minimum number of different kinds of assessment may be required.

> *Latest* information means that earlier assessments that are no longer relevant may be discarded and replaced by more recent evidence ... Whether to include an assessment item in the portfolio is a decision made by the teacher(s) on the basis of the contextual knowledge they have about the student. The ultimate aim is to represent the state of knowledge and capability as typically demonstrated by the student towards the end of the course. (Maxwell, 2004: 4–5).

The criteria for assessment, which are published so that students and parents as well as teachers can be familiar with them, describe what can be done in terms of grade descriptions. For example, one of the sub-categories of 'working scientifically' relates to planning and the criteria for this are set out at five levels or standards from A downwards:

Standard A: plans a range of scientific investigations of problems including many with elements of novelty and/or complexity

Standard B: plans a range of scientific investigations of problems including many with elements of novelty and/or complexity

Standard C: plans a range of scientific investigations of straightforward problems

Standard D: participates in planning some scientific investigations of straightforward problems

Standard E: participates in some aspects of planning scientific investigations of straightforward problems

Here the criteria for standards A and B are the same, but the judgment of planning is only one of several aspects of 'working scientifically' to be judged as a whole. The comparison of evidence with criteria involves judgments, not aggregation, and is an 'on-balance judgment' of best fit.

Moderation involves several stages, beginning with approval of the school's 'work plan' – the details of how the school intends to provide opportunities for students to meet the final criteria for assessment in a subject. Moderation of those subjects counting towards university selection involves external district panels, who review sample portfolios from schools and consider evidence that supports or challenges the schools' judgments. In turn a state panel reviews samples from districts and arbitrates difficult cases.

The openness of the on-going process of creating a portfolio means that at the end of a course there should be no surprises for either teachers or students. Further, the 'selective updating' and collection of 'fullest and latest' evidence allow poor starts, atypical performances, and earlier and temporary confusions (for whatever reason) to be ignored. Importantly, these processes facilitate the use of assessment to help learning for students to benefit from the feedback they receive on earlier assessments – and have the opportunity for self-assessment in deciding when to replace an earlier piece of work in their portfolio.

The Queensland experience supports the value of collaborative moderation not only in assuring reliable assessment but in providing professional development.

> The most powerful means for developing profession competence in assessment is the establishment of regular professional conversations among teachers about student performance (moderation conversations). This is best focussed on actual examples of student portfolios. Looking at actual examples and discussing the conclusions that can be drawn about the student's performance when compared to explicit standards sharpens teachers' judgment and builds knowledge and expertise about assessment more successfully than any other process. (Maxwell, 2004: 7)

It is important to note that while there are 'high stakes' attached to the certificate results for students, these are not linked to high stakes for the school, as school accountability is not directly linked to the certification results. Schools nevertheless are encouraged to use the data from the certification process for self-evaluation and school improvement.

Developmental Assessment

The use of progress maps is at the centre of Developmental Assessment, an approach developed in Australia for monitoring the progress of school students in an area of learning. A progress map is a description of the skills, knowledge and understanding in the sequence in which they typically appear. The maps are developed through a process of trial and refinement of initial maps, based on evidence of students' performance in relevant tests and teachers' experience.

Progress maps developed collaboratively across the Australian states and territories created the Australian Curriculum Profiles. These maps are in structure not unlike the statements of outcomes of learning in the National Curriculum and the Scottish 5–14 Guidelines in that they spell out, at eight levels, the progression in learning within strands within subject areas. However, this is only one form of progress map in the Australian scheme. It is not necessary for 'levels' to be identified for the map to have a formative use in guiding the next steps in learning. Moreover, the outcomes in the Australian profiles are expressed in general terms and need to be filled out by specific examples to be useful in formative assessment.

Some maps are constructed from the performance of students on relevant tests, using item-response modelling (van der Linden and Hambleton, 1996) to sequence the items in terms of their difficulty. Masters and Forster (1996) provide an example of a progress map for achievement in number developed from results for the 'number' strand of the Queensland Year 6 numeracy test. The map sets out statements of what students were successful in doing in a sequence of increasing achievement in number use. At the lower end is 'adds 2-digit whole numbers' and at the upper end 'represents common fractions on a number line'. In between are statements such as 'uses a calculator to subtract whole numbers' and 'continues number patterns', placed at points indicating their difficulty as found in test results for Year 6 students but not identified in terms of 'levels'. However, this approach confines the map to a description of skills and knowledge tested and needs to be supplemented using evidence from other sources.

Masters and Forster (1996) also give examples of maps developed in other ways, and how initial maps, either based on test performance or on an 'ideal' progression, are revised and refined through classroom trial. In the case of the development of spelling, the initial indicators of progress were clustered into five sequential phases: 'preliminary', 'semi-phonetic', 'phonetic', 'transitional' and 'independent'. Trials showed that the 'transitional' phase did not appear to represent a higher level of attainment than the 'phonetic', and so consideration was given to a revision and simplification of the sequence. Such examples underline the difficulties of identifying criteria against which progress can be judged, whatever the source of the evidence of performance. Indeed, Masters and Forster (1996) point out that a progress map is:

- not a description of a path that all children will follow (it describes typical progress but no two students learn exactly the same way);
- not a prescription for a learning sequence (it indicates the kinds of learning activities, but not a specific sequence);
- not based on the assumption that a child will demonstrate all skills and understanding below their estimated level of achievement (but probably most from below and some from above);
- not based on a single theory of learning (but on evidence from a range of sources);
- not a description of a purely 'natural' sequence of development (it is the result of the curriculum conventions as well as general mental development). (Adapted from Masters and Forster, 1996: 11)

An Example from the USA: The BEAR Assessment System

The Berkeley Evaluation and Assessment Research (BEAR) assessment system is based on an explicit model of learning and of progression in a particular area of study. The assessment is based on tasks or questions embedded in the learning material. The tasks and questions are systematically developed with both the learning model and subsequent inferences in mind, then tried out and the results of the trials systematically examined. The principles on which the system is based are that

- It should be related to a development perspective.
- There should be a match between what is taught and what is assessed.
- It should provide quality evidence, that is, evidence meeting the requirements of reliability, validity, fairness and lack of bias.
- It should serve formative and summative purposes in a manageable way.

The developmental perspective is implemented through specifying a set of 'progress variables'. As in the Australian progress maps, the idea of a progress variable

> is focused on the concept of progression or growth. Learning is conceptualized not simply as a matter of acquiring quantitatively more knowledge and skills, but as progress towards higher levels of competence as new knowledge is linked to existing knowledge and as deeper understandings are developed from and take the place of earlier understandings. (Wilson and Scalise, 2004: 5)

The description of progress is derived in part from research into the underlying cognitive structure of the domain and in part from professional opinion about what constitutes higher and lower levels of performance or competence, but is also, as in the case of the Australian profiles, informed by empirical research into how students respond to learning experiences and perform in practice. For instance, in the assessment of chemistry in higher education, the 'big ideas' are set out in a hierarchy of levels of sophistication. Success is identified at one of 12 points (four levels with three degrees of success within each). Examples of behaviours that students operating at these levels typically show, and of questions or tasks which would assess these levels, are set out in the BEAR framework for each concept and skill.

The principle of match between curriculum and assessment means that the frameworks for the assessment and for the teaching must be the same. The assessment tasks are developed at the same time as the curriculum material and include a wide range of activities which are both individual and group. Item-response modelling is used to provide quality control information (Adams and Wilson, 1996). The modelling enables the position of a student on a progress variable to be mapped.

> Maps can be used to record and track student progress and to illustrate the skills a student has mastered and those that the student is working on. By placing students' performance on the continuum defined by the map, instructors can demonstrate students' progress with respect to the goals and expectations of the course. The maps, therefore, are one tool to provide feedback on how students as a whole are progressing in the course. (Wilson and Scalise, 2004: 7)

Manageability is an important feature in the context of higher education, where large numbers of students are studying the course. There has to be a balance between using tasks that are readily scored or graded and the needs of students for formative feedback. Where it is appropriate, students can score classwork and map scores against progress variables, so that they can see for themselves the path towards learning goals.

Issues relating to quality of evidence provided mean that attention must be given to consistency in the use of the progress variables. A process of moderation, involving the discussion of student work by lecturers, teaching assistants, students and others involved in the course, is used to ensure that scores are interpreted in a similar way by all. This 'public' discussion of students' scores enables the fairness and consistency of the process to be examined by those involved, giving confidence in the results. Further, as Wilson and Scalise point out

> Moderation sessions also provide the opportunity for instructors to discuss implications of the assessment for their instruction, for example, by discussing ways to address common student mistakes or difficult concepts in the instructional sequence. This last aspect of moderation is perhaps the strongest influence of moderation on instruction. (Wilson and Scalise, 2004: 9)

Common Themes

A number of themes emerge from the brief description of systems where teachers' assessment is used for summarizing and reporting learning. Some key ones concern: the intention to promote the formative use of assessment at the same time as catering for summative assessment; the importance of criteria and particularly those describing development towards learning goals; the relevance of the application of a view of learning; and the wide benefits of moderation that involves group discussion of students' work.

While all the systems discussed in this chapter pay some attention to using information about students' progress formatively as well as for summative uses, this is a more prominent part of the rationale in Scotland, Wales and Northern Ireland, where evidence is explicitly drawn from regular work, than in the examples from Australia and the USA, where specific tasks and often tests are the sources of evidence. The use of assessment for learning is also advocated in England and indeed appears prominently in the various strategies and in documents and in CDs produced by the QCA, but there is a key difference in the action taken to support its implementation in practice. In Scotland, Wales and Northern Ireland, the new policies for students aged 3 to 14 acknowledge that the use of external tests, particularly when given high stakes through the use of results for school 'league tables' and target-setting, inhibits the implementation of formative assessment and needs to be removed if assessment really is to be used to support learning. Their new policies replace external tests with assessment by teachers based on regular work. This, of course, may include some tests and tasks devised or chosen by a teacher to focus on particular skills and knowledge, but not as the chief focus of the assessment as in the Queensland and BEAR systems.

It is in the context of regular work that assessment can be used to help learning and so ensure that summative assessment is not merely neutral in its impact on assessment for learning but can promote it. Opportunities for key features of formative assessment practice need to be built in, as some of the examples show. The decisions surrounding choice of evidence in the Queensland portfolios provide opportunity for teachers to give feedback to students, and for students to consider how far their work meets the criteria and what needs to be done further. In Scotland there is an explicit intention to enable students to learn from on-going assessment. Teachers constantly interpret the information they gather across a range of activities in relation to the descriptions of levels and report this to parents about twice a year. When a student is judged to have reached a level, and this judgment has been moderated in either of the ways proposed, the decision is reported at the appropriate time.

In all cases where teachers make judgments of students' achievement they need to compare the evidence with criteria that are sufficiently explicit to guide both the selection of relevant evidence and its interpretation, but yet are general enough to apply to different content and activities. This implies that they all fall into area 4 of the figure in Chapter 5 (see p. 71). There is a balance to be struck in this matter of the detail of goals and criteria if the assessment is to have formative as well as summative uses. This is taken up in the next chapter, looking at how these two uses can be effectively combined.

A feature of the criteria emphasised in the BEAR and developmental assessment approaches is that the criteria should be progressive; that is, based on some view of how development in certain skills and knowledge takes place. There has to be some basis for identifying progression, which is made explicit in the BEAR system in terms of a view of how learning takes place, but is left implicit in other statements of levels or progressive criteria. In practice, the criteria need to be informed both by empirical evidence, of students' performance and by theories of how learning takes place.

Moderation is key to confidence when summative assessment is based on teachers' judgments. Where it is missing, both teachers themselves and others consider the assessment to be of low reliability, perhaps justifiably. Moderation needs to be undertaken seriously, systematically and openly. When this is the case, as noted in several of the examples here, there are considerable benefits for teachers and students, not just in more reliable assessment, but through greater shared understanding of learning goals and how they can be achieved.

PART 3 Changing Assessment Practice and Policy

8 Teachers' assessment for and of learning

This chapter is concerned with how summative assessment can be practised so that it may be possible to say that all assessment has a role in helping learning. This is not the same, however, as saying that there is no distinction between formative and summative assessment, for the purposes they serve remain different. The distinction is not a sharp one; there are different degrees of formality in conducting both assessment for learning and assessment of learning. However, a consideration of the nature of what might be described as essentially 'formative' and essentially 'summative' assessment, at the start of this chapter, leads on to the identification of four important differences: in the detail of goals to which the assessment relates, the evidence and criteria used in making judgments, the attention to reliability and the participation of students.

Discussion of these differences draws attention to the unequal relationship between assessment for formative and summative purposes, that the results of summative assessment lack the detail to be used formatively, whilst the evidence used in formative assessment can be summarized for reporting. However, because of the different basis of judging evidence for the two purposes, it is essential to ensure that it is the evidence used in formative assessment and not the judgments that are summarized.

A model for using evidence both to help and to report on learning is proposed and illustrated with a brief example of summative assessment for internal purposes. This shows how evidence from on-going work relating to all kinds of goals can be summarized so that the practice of summative assessment not only avoids inhibiting formative assessment (as happens when there is frequent summative testing) but supports it by requiring the evidence that it depends upon. The conclusion highlights the value of teachers being responsible for summative assessment as the most effective way of ensuring that all assessment benefits learning.

Introduction

The relationship between formative assessment and summative assessment has been an underlying theme in several earlier chapters. What makes this of particular concern is that formative assessment, or assessment for learning, has proven and significant benefits for students' learning (Black and Wiliam, 1998a; Black et al., 2003), so it is essential that assessment for other purposes does not diminish the opportunities for it to be practised. The formative – summative assessment relationship, the focus in this chapter, is particularly important, since formative assessment is, in a sense, voluntary, in that it is possible to teach without it, whilst summative assessment is unavoidable because reports on students' learning have to be made and records kept at regular intervals; it cannot be avoided and neither can some impact on the use of formative assessment. If we want all assessment to help learning, then this has to guide decisions about how summative assessment is conducted.

The nature of the impact of summative assessment on the practice of formative assessment depends on how it is carried out. Earlier chapters have looked at the case against the use of high stakes testing on account of its impact on formative assessment, amongst other things. The discussion has made a case for using teachers' judgments based on evidence collected during teaching as the basis for summative assessment. As well as providing more valid reports of learning, this has the advantage that the evidence can be used formatively as well as being summarized for reporting purposes.

Moving on from these arguments, this chapter considers what this means in practice. What are the procedures that enable formative assessment and summative assessment to work together? The starting point has to be a closer look at the nature of formative assessment and summative assessment. This reveals differences in several aspects that need to be taken into account in ensuring that both purposes are most effectively served. A model of how to serve both purposes is proposed and illustrated with an example of evidence used formatively and for internal summative assessment.

Assessment for Learning (Formative Assessment)

Empirical investigations of classroom assessment have been the subject of several reviews of research, principally those by Natriello (1987), Kulik and Kulik (1987), Crooks (1988), Black (1993) and Black and Wiliam (1998a). The last of these has attracted a good deal of attention world-wide due largely to its dissemination in the form of a short booklet, *Inside the Black Box* (Black and Wiliam, 1998b), and several papers for professional and lay audiences, but also because of the authors' attempt to quantify the positive impact on learning of using assessment for learning. They estimated that the gains in learning were large enough to 'improve performances of pupils in GCSE by between one and two grades' (Black and Wiliam, 1998b: 4). Further, they reported that 'improved formative assessment helps the (so-called) low attainers more than the rest, and so reduces the spread of attainment whilst also raising it overall' (ibid).

But what does 'improved formative assessment' mean in practice? The research shows that there are several key components of formative assessment:

- Feedback to the students that provides advice on how to improve or move forward, and avoids making comparisons with other students.
- Students understanding the goals of their work and having a grasp of what is good quality work.
- Students being involved in self-assessment so that they take part in identifying what they need to do to improve or move forward.
- Students engaged in expressing and communicating their understandings and skills, initiated by teachers' open and person-centred questions.
- Dialogue between teacher and students that encourages reflection on their learning.
- Teachers using information about on-going learning to adjust teaching so that all students have opportunity to learn.

It is easy to see that these components are inter-related and that making changes in one only will not necessarily cause changes in students' achievements. There is an essential 'whole' here – a classroom ethos that encourages engagement and autonomy in learning combined with creative and learner-centred teaching. It is useful to explore how the parts fit together into the whole, as this helps in identifying what is needed to create synergy between formative and summative assessment.

Formative assessment is essentially a continuing and repeated cycle of events in which teacher and students use information from on-going activities to determine the next steps in learning and how to take them. Figure 8.1 brings together the components of using assessment for learning. The activities A, B, and C are directed towards the goals of the lesson, or series of lessons, on a topic. These goals, shared with the students by the teacher, are expressed in *specific* terms; for example in a science lesson, 'to plan and to carry out an investigation of the conditions preferred by woodlice'. The students' work in activity A, directed to achieving the goals, provides an opportunity for both teacher and students to obtain evidence relating to the achievement of these goals. To interpret the evidence both need to know what 'good planning' means, so students must have some understanding of the criteria to apply when assessing their work (for example, is the planned investigation taking account of all relevant variables? What evidence will be gathered and how?) The judgment leads to a decision about the relevant next steps and so on to activity B, which is the result of deciding how to improve or move on.

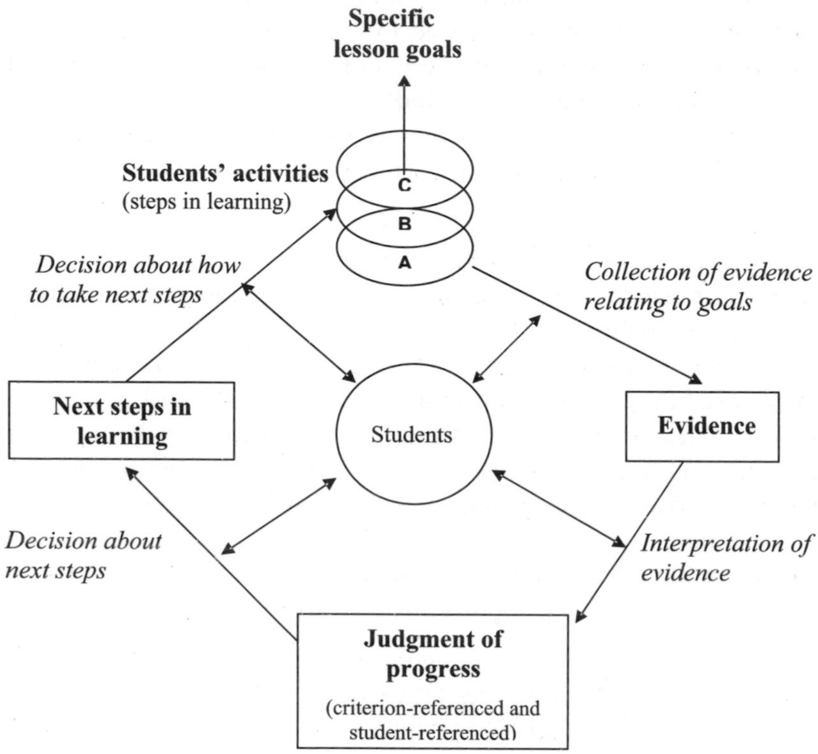

Figure 8.1 Assessment for learning as a cycle of events (adapted from Harlen, 2006a)

The students are at the centre of the process, since it is they who do the learning. The two-headed arrows linking students to the various parts of the assessment cycle indicate that students both receive feedback from the teacher and also provide information and participate in decisions where appropriate.

In formative assessment, judgments about progress and decisions about next steps take into account the circumstances, past learning and effort of individual students, as well as what they are able to do in relation to the goals of the work at a particular time. Thus the judgments are both student-referenced and criterion-referenced. As long as no comparisons are made between students, which in formative assessment should not be the case, this approach supports learning far more than applying the same standards to all students. To do that can lead to the demotivation of lower-achieving students, who are constantly judged by standards too far beyond their reach.

The actions indicated by the boxes in Figure 8.1 are not 'stages' in a lesson or necessarily the result of conscious decisions made by the teacher. They represent the thinking involved in focusing on what and how students are learning and using this to help further learning. In some cases it may be possible for teacher and students together to decide on immediate action. In other cases, the teacher may take note of what is needed and provide it at a later time. Implementing formative assessment means that not everything in a lesson can be planned in advance. By definition, if students' current learning is to be taken into account, some decisions will depend on what that learning is. Some ideas can be anticipated from teachers' experience and from research findings built into curriculum materials, but not all. What the teacher needs is not prescribed lesson content but a set of strategies to deploy according to what is found to be appropriate on particular occasions.

Bringing these points together, some key characteristics of assessment used to help learning are that it:

- can only be conducted by teachers, in collaboration with students, since they can gather information from on-going activities;
- is an integral and continuous part of teaching; it is cyclical, with each decision building on earlier ones;
- relates to the achievement of specific goals from one lesson or a series of lessons;
- leads to action that supports further learning;
- relates to learning goals of all kinds;
- involves students in assessing their work and deciding their next steps;
- is not a measurement; it does not lead to grades or levels.

Assessment of Learning – Summative Assessment

When assessment is used for summative purposes, the chief aim is to summarize what has been learned. The process of gathering and interpreting the information may have some impact on learning, or the outcome may be used in planning future teaching, but the assessment is not carried out primarily with these uses in mind; its rationale is to report achievement at a particular time. However, the possibility of these other uses implies that there is no hard and fast dividing line between formative and summative assessment. An informal classroom test might well be used by a teacher as a quick assessment of what has been learned in a topic in order to plan future lessons and as feedback to students about what they can and cannot do. Students may mark their own or one another's answers in order to ensure this direct feedback. What we seem to have, rather than a dichotomy between formative and summative purposes, is a dimension of assessment purposes from the purely formative to the purely summative. In between these extremes are various assessment activities that could be described as 'formal formative' (mainly formative with some summative use) and 'informal summative' (mainly summative but with some feedback into learning) (Harlen, 2006b).

In order to identify the differences between assessment for and of learning, we are considering the extreme ends of this dimension. So this means looking at the more formal summative purpose, where the assessment is intended to result in a valid and reliable report on the achievements of each individual student. The process is represented in Figure 8.2.

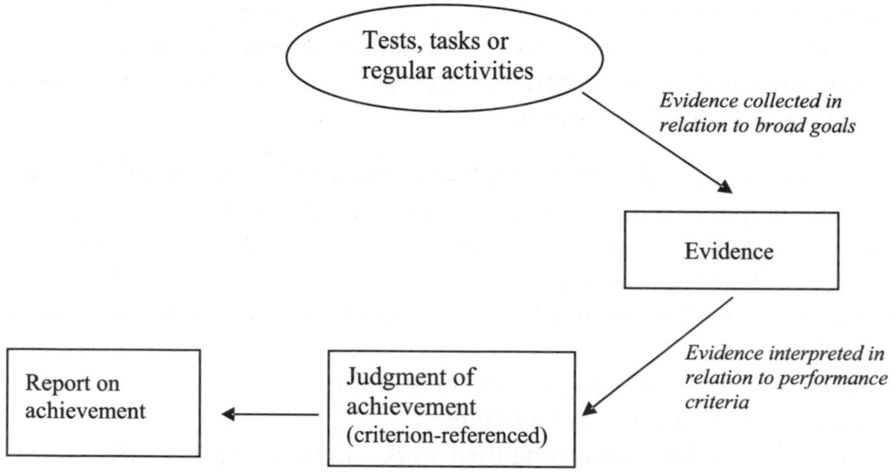

Figure 8.2 Assessment of learning (adapted from Harlen, 2006a)

Figure 8.2 shows current practice in which evidence may be drawn from a range of activities and/or from special tasks, tests or examinations. This evidence relates to broad goals (for instance, the development of 'investigative skills') combining a range of specific learning goals (of which one might be planning the woodlice investigation and others would relate to conducting and using evidence in an investigation).

When external tests or examinations are used as a basis for the evidence then there is no role for students except as a source of evidence. As noted before, tests and examinations are often used when the decisions may affect students' future learning, such as when making decisions about grouping or selection for certain schools or for higher and further education, because they are considered to be fair and reliable. They involve carefully controlled, and usually pre-trialled, procedures for collecting and grading evidence. However, the evidence and arguments discussed in Chapters 2 and 4 indicate that the extent to which they give a valid account of learning and the accuracy of the judgments is limited by the small sample of learning that can be assessed in tests of reasonable length. Moreover, the processes of selecting the items that are included also limits the range of cognitive skills that is included. This results in a mismatch between the wide range of goals of education that are extolled in curriculum policy documents and those that are assessed and reported in practice. For these reasons it is important to consider alternative ways of assessing students' learning for summative purposes.

When the process is in the hands of the teacher, there is the potential for gathering information about a range of different learning goals including, for instance, affective outcomes, problem solving, creative, critical and other higher-level thinking skills. But there remains the obligation to ensure that judgments are reliable and based on the same criteria for all students. Using student-referenced criteria for this purpose would be a source of bias or error. Thus some processes of moderation have to be included in the procedures. When the procedures for assessment and moderation are open to all concerned then there is some opportunity for student self-assessment. These factors are discussed in the next section.

In summary, some key characteristics of summative assessment are that it

- may be based on teachers' judgments or external tests, or a combination of these;
- is not a cycle taking place as a regular part of learning, but only at times when achievement is to be reported;
- relates to the achievement of broad goals expressed in general terms;
- provides results expressed in terms of publicly available criteria for grades or levels;
- judges all students by the same criteria;
- requires some measures to assure reliability;
- may, in some circumstances, provide opportunities for student self-assessment.

Using Evidence for Formative and Summative Assessment

Formative assessment has to be in the hands of the teacher who, we argue, therefore already has all the evidence needed for summative assessment. In making use of this evidence, there are potential difficulties, as Black and Wiliam report in their review of classroom assessment:

> ... tension between formative and summative assessment arises when teachers are responsible for both functions: there has been a debate between those who draw attention to the difficulties in combining the two roles ... and those who argue that it can be done and indeed must be done to escape the dominance of external summative testing.... (Black and Wiliam, 1998a: 19)

In this section we consider how the two roles may be combined in practice and the difficulties turned into advantages. The starting point is the two lists of characteristics of formative assessment and of summative assessment. These show some key differences in the processes involved that ought to be taken into account if evidence from on-going activities is to be used both to help learning and to report on it. The main points refer to the specificity of the goals, the evidence and criteria used in making judgments, the attention to reliability and the participation of students.

Specificity of Goals

Lesson goals are specific to the development of particular concepts, skills and attitudes required in studying particular content, and learning activities are planned to help achieve these goals. In formative assessment, teachers gather and interpret information in relation to where the students are in their progress to achieving the goals. The interpretation is in terms of what to do to help further learning, not what level or grade a child has reached. An understanding of the nature of progression is needed to decide the next steps.

In summative assessment, the purpose is to report on the overall achievement in relation to broad goals. The individual lesson goals are far too detailed to be useful for this purpose. For example, the goals of a specific lesson might include an understanding of how the structure of particular plants or animals is suited to the places where they are found. This will contribute to an understanding of how living organisms in general are suited to their habitats, but achieving this understanding will depend on looking at a variety of organisms, which will be the subject of other lessons with their own specific goals. Similarly, skills such as planning a scientific investigation are developed not in one lesson, but in different contexts in different lessons.

If information from on-going activities is to be used for summative assessment, there has to be some way of summarizing in terms of development towards the broader goals used as headings for reporting progress. The lesson goals are of course related to the broad goals, but moving from judgments made in relation to detailed goals and on to the more general goals is not a simple aggregation of judgments. This is because of the difference in the basis of judgments made in formative and summative assessment, which we now consider.

Evidence and Criteria Used in Making Judgments

In formative assessment judgments are made by interpreting evidence from on-going activities in terms of the progress of individual students towards goals, that is, they are student-referenced as well as criterion-referenced. So it is important to distinguish between the *evidence* and the *interpretation of that evidence* when considering assessment for different purposes. Evidence used to report on learning in terms of achievement of broader goals must be evaluated according only to the criteria relating to those goals, and must not be influenced by student-related considerations. Thus the evidence used in formative assessment can also be used for summative reporting, providing it is *reinterpreted* against criteria that are the same for all students. This means that if the information already gathered and used to help learning is to be used for summative assessment, it must be reviewed against the broader criteria that define levels or grades. This involves finding the 'best fit' between the evidence gathered about each student and one of the reporting levels.

The process of reinterpretation of evidence from on-going activity may seem to involve the retention and review of a large amount of material. In some subject areas this would be unmanageable and indeed it is not necessary. But the relevant period of time is not the whole Key Stage or whole two year GCSE course, but the time between reports on students' progress, which usually take place two or three times each year. The end-of-stage and course assessment is thus built up during the stage or course.

What is required when it comes to making judgments for reporting is the best evidence at that time. This can be accumulated gradually by retaining what is best at any time in a folder, or other form of portfolio, and replacing pieces with better evidence as it is produced. Whilst it is important to base the summative judgment on evidence from a range of activities and not judge from one task, there is no point in including work that no longer reflects what students are capable of producing. Moreover, such an approach enables students to have a role in their summative assessment by taking part in the selection of items for the folder or portfolio, a process for which they need some understanding of the broad goals and quality criteria by which their work will be judged.

Attention to Reliability

Although, as noted in Chapter 4, it would be true to say that any assessment will be more useful the more reliable or accurate it is, in formative assessment reliability is not of major concern, as it is in summative assessment. In formative assessment it is far more important that the assessment is based on the most valid evidence than that this is compromised in the pursuit of high reliability. There are two reasons for this. The first is that in formative assessment the evidence is gathered and used by the teacher who is, therefore, aware of how sound a basis there is for making a judgment. It is not as if the person receiving and using the information is at a distance from the work that is assessed, as is generally the case in external summative assessment. The second reason refers to the cyclic nature of the process of formative assessment, which means that repeated observations will soon reveal errors in evidence or interpretation and the on-going situation provides opportunities to adjust decisions about next steps.

The position is different in summative assessment, where the individual pieces of evidence are buried in the overall judgment and the result is intended to inform other teachers, parents, and so on, who have to trust the accuracy of the information they are given. Then steps have to be taken to achieve the level of reliability appropriate to use of the information. Ways of doing this have been discussed in Chapter 5.

The Participation of Students

Giving students some role in assessing their learning is central to promoting learning autonomy, which 'would seem to be the most secure foundation for lifelong learning' (Black et al., 2006a: 130). In the context of formative assessment, self-assessment focuses on the lesson goals which are often 'tailored' to the progress and abilities of individual students. This means that a student who succeeds in achieving a less advanced goal can feel the same degree of satisfaction as one whose goal is more advanced. Both are motivated by their achievement to make further effort. But what happens when the time comes for reporting achievement and all have to be judged by the same criteria?

When summative assessment takes the form of tests or examinations in which self-assessment has no role, then the result is likely to bring awareness of differences which are interpreted by the lower achievers as failure. More likely, practice tests may have already made this clear to some and these students may have written off any chance of success and ceased to make an effort. This learned helplessness ensures that these students' prophesy of failure will be fulfilled.

So, given that self-assessment can support self-esteem and promote further learning in formative assessment, could it not have the same role in summative assessment? It is far easier to see this as a possibility when the summative assessment is carried out by teachers and based on the regular work of students than when it is on the basis of tests or tasks that they are given, unseen, solely for the purpose of assessment. The selection of evidence for the summative assessment, as suggested above, can be carried out by the teacher in collaboration with the student. To make this selection, the student needs to have some idea of the summative assessment criteria at different levels. Sharing these criteria, in terms that are meaningful for students, helps them to know what they are aiming for overall. It is important that they see this information as helping them and not labelling them.

The process of summative assessment needs to be handled carefully because, as with any assessment, it has an emotional impact. Lower-achieving students particularly need to be helped to interpret summative assessment so that

> when they don't have skills or knowledge, or they're behind other students, this is not a sign of a deep, shameful deficit. It's a sign that they need to study harder or find new learning strategies. (Dweck, 2000: 129)

It is important, too, for this preparation for summative assessment to take place only as necessary for summative reporting, allowing assessment at other times to be concerned with helping students to achieve lesson goals, which ultimately leads to the achievement of broader goals.

A Model for Using Evidence Both to Help and to Report on Learning

With these differences in the characteristics of assessment for formative and summative purposes in mind, we now turn to the issue of how to create synergy between assessment for and of learning. Theoretically there are two starting points leading to two questions. Can evidence used in summative assessment be used to help learning? Can evidence collected for formative purposes be used for summative assessment?

Starting with the first of these, there are examples of the formative use of summative assessment given by Black et al. (2003). These practices include: using test items to enable students to review their understanding and help their revision; involving students in setting test questions and marking schemes; and using students to mark their own and others' tests and so diagnose areas of difficulty. These can all be described as 'informal summative' approaches and are only feasible in the context of teachers being in control of the summative assessment. Although it is possible to use some external tests and examinations in this way, by obtaining marked scripts and discussing them with students, in practice this rarely happens, if only because these examinations come at the end of a stage and students are moving on elsewhere. Even when teachers use tests to feed back into learning, there are severe limitations. Black et al. (2003) themselves point out the danger of 'teaching to the test' and substituting evidence that can be used formatively with frequently-gathered summative evidence.

The ten principles of assessment for learning (ARG, 2002b) provide useful criteria for judging whether assessment in a particular context has a truly formative purpose. For instance:

- Does it focus on how students learn?
- Is it sensitive and constructive?
- Does it foster motivation?
- Does it promote understanding of goals and criteria?

- Does it help learners to know how to improve?
- Does it develop the capacity for self-assessment?
- Does it recognize all educational achievements?

It is not difficult to see that a process that starts from summative assessment is unlikely to meet these criteria, unless formative use is built into the procedures. This could be said to be the case in the Queensland portfolio system, outlined in Chapter 7, but it could not be said of the use of tests and examinations, even when these are teacher-made.

Turning to the second question of using formative evidence summatively, we have already argued that this is possible provided that the evidence used formatively is reinterpreted in terms of reporting criteria common to all students. We now look in more detail at what is involved in putting this into practice. Figure 8.3 attempts to represent the main processes and relationships involved.

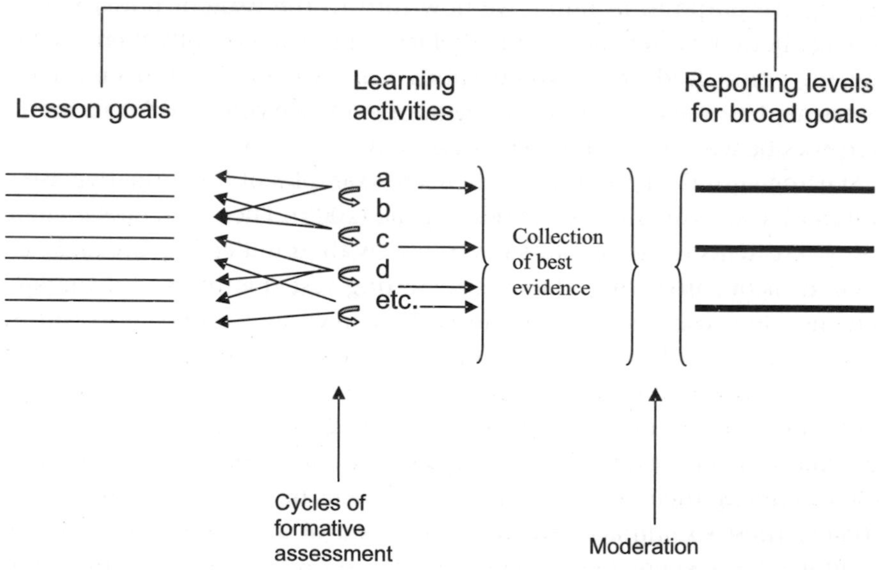

Figure 8.3 Using evidence from learning activities for both formative and summative purposes

The origin of evidence for both purposes is the series of relevant learning activities represented by a, b, c, d, and so on. The arrows to the left of the activities represent the relationship between the evidence from these activities and the detailed lesson goals. Cycles of formative assessment use this evidence to help learning towards these goals. Students have a central part in these cycles, as indicated in Figure 8.1, for which they need to have an operational understanding of the goals and of the criteria of quality to apply in judging their work.

The arrows to the right represent the use of evidence for summative assessment. Not all the evidence will be relevant at the time of the summative reporting, some having been superseded by better evidence. It is in making this selection that students can be involved and come to understand the broader goals to which the detailed goals of their work are related (indicated by the linking line between the two sets of goals). In making the selection the aim is to reflect where the student has reached at the time of reporting, not some notion of progress over the period covered by the report or an average performance over that period. The judgment of the selected best evidence in relation to reporting levels is a process of finding the 'best fit' – usually by scanning the criteria of the most likely level and of those immediately above and below. The process and the results require some moderation to guard against different interpretations of the criteria or bias through taking into account information not relevant to the criteria.

The Process in Action

As an example of this dual use of evidence, take a series of science lessons in which Year 8 students were studying the transfer of heat energy through different materials. At one point they were investigating the insulating properties of various materials that could be used to make coats. They were provided with metal containers in which they could put water to represent a 'body' and pieces of fabric to wrap around the outside of the containers. Thermometers were placed in the water to measure changes in the 'body' temperature. But there were several decisions to make in setting up the investigations. What should the initial temperature of the water inside the container be? Would it give useful results to carry out the investigation in the warm laboratory instead of outside in the cold? How to make sure that the comparison was fair? Some of these decisions required the students to apply what they knew about conduction and other ways of transferring heat energy, whilst others required an understanding of how to make fair comparisons.

While they were planning what they would do, the teacher drew their attention to the list of things to consider in planning an investigation – a list which had been developed from an earlier discussion and which was in their folders. The teacher observed their actions and listened to their talk as they planned and carried out their investigations, occasionally asking groups for explanations of their reasons for how they were doing certain things. At the stage of reporting on their findings, there was further opportunity for the teacher to gather evidence that could be used to help in developing the students' understanding of how heat energy is transferred and their enquiry skills.

Thus, during the lesson, the teacher responded to what she saw and heard by raising questions to provoke a rethinking of decisions; asking for justification of statements or actions; asking for explanations of how certain parts of the investigation would help them achieve their goal. In other words, the teacher was using evidence formatively to help learning. She also made notes of the help that some students had required so that this could be followed up in future lessons.

Then, at the end of the year, when it was necessary to report progress in terms of levels achieved, the teacher reviewed the evidence from this and other science lessons. For both the conceptual goals and the enquiry skills goals, evidence from different specific activities had to be brought together so as to form an overall judgment for each student about where he or she had reached in development of the 'bigger' ideas and more generalized skills. In preparation for this the teacher made time available for the students to look through their folders and compare their later accounts of investigations with their earlier ones, in terms of how evidence had been collected and used to reach a result and an explanation of that result. They then picked out the best examples of work with these features.

By providing lesson time for this the teacher was able to talk with individuals to ensure that the selection criteria were understood and appropriately applied. She then reviewed the evidence against the criteria for reporting levels of attainment, in this case descriptions for Levels 4, 5 and 6 of 'scientific enquiry' and of 'physical processes' in the English National Curriculum. The results were reviewed by the head of department and the evidence for a sample of three students was discussed at a departmental moderation meeting.

Conclusion

In terms of the aim of making sure that all assessment has a role in helping learning, one of the key benefits of operating a process such as that modelled in Figure 8.3 is the reflection on learning that is involved in reviewing students' work and in moderation. In these activities not only are meanings of criteria and levels clarified and agreement reached about judgments of students' learning, but teachers face the reality of assessment as an essentially imprecise process. It may well be that, for the higher-achieving students, the decision is straightforward; it may also be all too evident for the lower achievers, but for the great majority there will be some evidence fitting more than one level, and some missing evidence adding to the uncertainty. In such circumstances the apparent precision of a test score may seem a better alternative – until, that is, the realization comes that the meaning of the result is equally uncertain because it is based on a small sample of work and has all the other disadvantages discussed in Chapter 4.

It is important to recognize and accept the consequences for assessment of unevenness in students' development and the time it takes for progress to be made towards broad conceptual understanding and key skills. It is no accident that different 'levels' in national curricula are about two years apart. The practice of dividing these levels into 'sub-levels' or 'points', so that supposed progress can be reported more frequently, has severe disadvantages. It moves the criteria away from being based on what is known about how students learn and the development of ideas and skills. It also creates a need for frequent checks on progress, often called formative because they are frequent, but which are in fact a series of summative assessments.

9 Summative assessment within the assessment system

This chapter attempts to draw together the main points introduced in earlier chapters. It begins by reviewing the arguments relating to the negative consequences of using high stakes summative assessment to evaluate teachers and schools. The discussion leads to the conclusion that systems of school accountability should not rely solely, or even mainly, on the data derived from summative assessment of students. Such data should be reported, and interpreted, in the context of the broad set of indicators of school effectiveness. In relation to monitoring standards of students' achievements at the system level, the data should be derived from a wider base of evidence than test results from individual students.

Other factors are considered that may need to be changed if a more valid, reliable, fair and cost-effective system of summative assessment is to be introduced. The main points relate to: changes in the curriculum and pedagogy that are both required and encouraged; a need for developmental criteria or level descriptions that reflect progression in various dimensions of learning; the provision of well-designed tasks assessing skills and understanding, which can help teachers to make judgments across the full range of learning goals; the need for summative assessment procedures to be transparent and for some rethinking of the use of teachers' time that recognizes the importance to learning of effective teacher-based assessment. Finally, some implications are offered for all involved in education policy and practice.

Introduction

Although this book is concerned with one part of an assessment system – summative assessment – this has to be considered within the context of the other components that make up a whole system. The interconnections among the components and between them and the social and cultural context in which they operate give rise to complex issues. In this final chapter various parts of a system, many of which have been considered separately in earlier chapters, are brought together and some issues are revisited.

The case for change in systems that depend largely on tests and examinations for the summative assessment of students was made in Chapters 2–4. This made clear that changes must go beyond the procedures for assessment of learning if the intended advantages are to be realized. In particular, the uses of information about students' achievements for evaluation of schools and system monitoring need to be changed to avoid the assessment, however it is carried out, having a narrowing impact on the curriculum and pedagogy. These uses are discussed in the first section of this chapter.

The second part picks up some of the issues that have to be addressed if changes are to be made and if assessment of learning by teachers is to match up to the standards of validity and reliability that are necessary and, indeed, possible. These issues include the relationship of assessment to the curriculum, how assessment criteria are defined in the curriculum, the role of tests and special tasks in the context of teachers' assessment and the use of teachers' time. The importance of ensuring that the procedures of summative assessment protect the practice of formative assessment is a recurring theme.

Finally, we propose some implications of making changes of the kind discussed for the various players in the educational system: local and national policy makers, inspectors and advisers of assessment, school management, teachers, and providers of initial teacher education and professional development.

Uses and Abuses of Student Assessment Information: Accountability and System Monitoring

The various components that make up an assessment system are concerned with how information is generated and used for a range of purposes. These components include: helping learning and fostering deeper engagement with it (formative assessment or assessment for learning); keeping records or making decisions about individual students (summative assessment or assessment of learning); reporting to parents, students and other teachers; evaluation of teachers, schools, local/district authorities; year-on-year comparison of students' achievements for monitoring national or regional standards. The interconnection between one component of a system and another has been noted, particularly in relation to how the procedures for summative assessment can have an impact on the practice of formative assessment. Through considering the requirements in relation to the properties introduced in Chapter 1 – validity, reliability, avoidance of negative impact and efficient use of resources – a case has been made for a change away from the emphasis that exists in many systems on using external tests and examinations, and towards making more and better use of assessment by teachers.

However, it has to be recognized that it is not the use of tests and examinations alone that leads to the narrowing impact on students' learning experiences and inhibits the use of assessment to help learning. The high stakes added to students' assessment results by using them as the sole measure of the effectiveness of teachers, schools and the system as a whole also play a significant part in the impact that assessment has. We might well ask about what gains are intended by using test results in this way, when this use is perceived as unfair and distorts students' school experience (Boyle and Bragg, 2006). The rationale for this policy is that 'testing drives up standards'. However, there is no evidence to support this and indeed plenty to suggest that any rises in tests scores are due to teaching to the test. Here we summarize just some of this evidence.

Tymms (2004) reported an exhaustive review of test results in England from 1995 to 2003. He made reference to data on test results from nine sources, in addition to the statutory national tests for pupils at age 11 and 13. The data from five key sources (including international surveys of achievements) were analysed to show year-on-year changes. The pattern found in national test results for 11 year olds was a rise over the first five years (1995–1999) followed by no change from 2000 to 2003. The pattern was the same for mathematics and English. While some other data supported a rise from 1995–1999, it was noted that the data from the Trends in Mathematics and Science Surveys (TIMSS) showed no rise in mathematics over this period.

Tymms (2004) identified several reasons why standards of tests may have changed over this time (mainly related to how cut-off scores for levels are determined when tests change from year to year) and how this could have accounted for some of the reported increase. At that time the effect of teaching test technique (new to pupils of this age in 1995) and of teaching to the test are very likely to have accounted for a good deal of the initial change, as they have in other test regimes. For example, in the USA, Linn found 'a pattern of early gains followed by a levelling off' (Linn, 2000: 6) to be typical across states where high stakes tests are used.

Gradually, the case for claiming that standards of achievement have increased since the introduction of national testing is demolished. So the situation is that we really cannot tell from national test results what is happening to national standards. Claims that there has been a rise in standards due to the introduction of various initiatives and innovations in the curriculum, and indeed to the introduction of testing itself, cannot be substantiated.

However, removing the high stakes added by using students' results for school accountability and for setting school and national targets would not make tests and examinations any more valid or fair in relation to what is assessed. That part of the case for moving to greater use of teachers' asessment would remain. But since the problems of using student assessment results for accountability apply also to results from teachers' assessment, the benefits of moving away from use of tests are likely to be reduced unless there are changes in these other parts of the assessment system. It is important, therefore, to look in more detail at these uses of students' assessment results. We can do this by referring again to the required properties of assessment in relation to these uses.

Accountability

Being accountable means being responsible for one's actions and being able to explain to stakeholders why and how certain things were done or why they were not done. Schools are now expected to communicate and explain their philosophy, aims and policies to the wider community. As with the purposes of assessment where the focus is on an individual student, so the use of aggregate data about the performance of groups of students can be either formative, helping an institution to improve, or summative, providing a judgment that is used for decision making. Also, as in the case of individual assessment, there is greater value from the process when those being held accountable are involved in it as opposed to following externally devised procedures.

People can only be held accountable for actions or outcomes over which they have control. In the context of students' learning, teachers can be held accountable for what they do in the classroom, what learning opportunities they provide and the help they give to students, and so on. They are not necessarily responsible for whether externally-prescribed learning outcomes are achieved, since this depends on many other factors over which the teacher does not have control, such as the students' prior learning and the many out-of-school influences and conditions that affect their learning. These factors need to be taken into account, both by teachers in setting and working towards their goals for students' learning and by those who hold teachers accountable for students' achievements.

For teachers, accountability operates at a number of levels: to themselves, at the individual level, as part of self-evaluation; to the school and its parents and governors, as part of its internal evaluation; to the local authority, as part of external school evaluation; and so on to the national level. The effect of accountability at each of these levels depends on:

- The type of information that is taken into account (for instance, varying from student achievement data only to a range of relevant information about learning processes, contexts and outcomes).
- The criteria used in judging effectiveness (for instance, in relation to student achievement, varying from whether externally-prescribed targets

in a narrow range of knowledge and skills have been met to whether achievement in a range of academic and non-academic areas meets expectations).
- The action that follows the judgment of effectiveness (for instance, varying from sanctions or rewards to supportive action to correct areas of weakness).

When sanctions or rewards are attached to the results, attention is inevitably focused on maximizing the outcomes that are assessed, which in turn acquire 'high stakes'. The consequence is to focus teaching and the curriculum on what is assessed, narrowing students' learning opportunities. But as noted earlier, this can happen whether the evidence of students' achievements is derived from tests or teachers' judgments. For a more positive impact, accountability is best when based on information about a range of student achievements and learning activities, judged by reference to the context and circumstances of a school, and used positively to improve students' opportunities for learning.

It follows from these arguments that the information used in accountability should include, in addition to data on students' achievements, information about the curriculum and teaching methods and relevant aspects of students' backgrounds and of their learning histories. Various school self-evaluation guidelines provide some good examples of what this means (SEED, 2002; DfES and OfSTED, 2004; Estyn, 2004a and 2004b). Here we focus on the nature and sources of the student assessment data that are used.

Validity

It is important for the student achievement information used for accountability to reflect the full range of goals, both academic and non-academic. Tests, whether teacher-made or external, are unlikely to do this. Since the information is not used to make decisions about or to report on individuals, it need not be collected from all the students in a class. So whilst it may be convenient to use existing data, such as from internal or external tests, it will be more meaningful to gather evidence of a wider range from a sample of students. This can be done, for instance, by a teacher or a visitor interviewing and reviewing the work of a few students so that their understanding and affective outcomes can be probed. Also it may be more informative to report on the progress of groups of students, such as the lowest- and highest-achieving students, than on the average of the whole class.

Reliability

The question in relation to reliability is whether the information about student achievement used in holding a teacher or school accountable is sufficiently accurate for sound and fair judgments to be made. One reason for using the results of tests and examination for this purpose is that these are assumed to have high reliability. Such assumptions, as noted in Chapter 4, are not justified. Teachers' judgments can, when moderated, provide more accurate information than external tests because they can cover a much wider range of outcomes and so provide a more complete picture of students' achievements.

Impact

When the information is derived from summative assessment carried out for other purposes, there is the danger that it is not well matched to the purpose of accountability. For instance, there are multiple disadvantages if external test or examination results are used and a school is held accountable for whether a specified target percentage of students reach a certain level. The results are unlikely to reflect the full range of educational outcomes which a school strives for and for which it should be held accountable. Moreover, as we have mentioned earlier, to reach the target attention is focused on those students who are close to the required level, with less attention given to those who are either too far below or are already above the target level, and for all students most attention is given to the narrow requirements of passing the test or examination.

Thus framing accountability in terms of targets for student achievement, or position in a league table of schools based on test and examination results, distorts the actions of those held accountable in ways that may not be intended and are not in the best interests of the students. It means that neither is there genuine information about actions for which teachers and schools should be held responsible nor a positive impact that enables performance to be improved. If, instead of blanket testing, the work of a sample of students is considered in greater depth, with appropriate moderation, the outcome can have diagnostic value for the teachers and school, leading to improvement in practice.

Resources

Accountability of teachers and schools to students, parents and the community is an essential part of professional practice. There is inevitably a cost in time spent in collecting, analysing and communicating information, whatever the type and range used. When the information used encompasses a wide range of students' academic and non-academic activities and achievements, the process of giving an account has formative as well as summative value. The cost in terms of teachers' time is probably greater than when the process involves only the collection of existing data from external tests or examinations, but the value is much greater to the users of such information and to the schools and teachers themselves.

System Monitoring

Monitoring implies the regular collection of information in order to detect changes over time. In the context of education it refers to changes in levels of student achievement and is usually associated with whether 'standards' are rising, falling or remaining steady. Although the evidence used includes student achievement, the purpose is to inform policy and practice decisions and not to make judgments or decisions about individual students. Monitoring can concern a range of aspects of practice, but attention here is confined to the role that student performance takes.

Monitoring student performance can be undertaken in relation to a small group, a class, a year group in a school or across a local authority or the whole national system. It generally requires equivalent evidence to be gathered about different cohorts of students at a particular stage or age, so that, say, the performance of 13 year olds at one time can be compared with the performance of 13 year olds at a later time. Since there are many differences between successive cohorts of students of the same age, comparisons for small groups have very low reliability. Monitoring at the school level is best undertaken within the context of self-evaluation, where other information needed to interpret student assessment data is also collected. Even at the system level, which is our concern here, a change from one year to the next is unlikely to be meaningful; trends over several years provide more useful information.

Whereas in gathering evidence for summative assessment of individual students any test is acknowledged to be only a sample of the domain, in the case of system monitoring it is the *subject domain* that is being assessed rather than the students. To serve its purpose, the information gathered for system monitoring should include a wide range of outcomes in the subject domain being monitored. Only then can trends be safely used for informing policy and practice decisions. For example, it is important to know whether an increase in performance in one aspect, say computational arithmetic, is accompanied by an increase or decrease in other aspects. The implication of this is that evidence is needed of a greater range of performance than can reasonably be accommodated by testing each and every student. However, since the purpose is not to judge the achievement of individual students, the items in a domain can be spread across several students, as long as equivalent samples of students are given each item.

Validity

The value of system monitoring depends on the range of information that is collected. The obvious approach of collecting test results from national tests, taken by every student in a cohort, reduces the information to a small sample of the subject domain that any one student can reasonably be expected to provide. Validity is further reduced by basing the information only on the results of tests that are designed to give reliable information about individuals, and thus are focused on aspects that can be scored most easily and objectively. For valid monitoring, a wider range of evidence is needed, derived from observation of skills in action as well as assessment of products. Without this, decisions about policy and practice will not be based on relevant information about students' achievements of the goals that are in theory supported by government policy.

The validity of assessment of skills, which is generally low for any one task due to content dependence, can be increased by using a number of tasks that between them cover a variety of content. As there is no need for every student to be given every item or task, the number of tasks need not be limited to what a single student can undertake. Nor does every student need to be involved; all that is needed is an adequate sample of the population being monitored. Sampling of this kind, where only a small proportion of students is selected and each only takes a sample of the full range of items, is used in international surveys (such as the OECD's PISA and the IEA surveys such as TIMSS) and in national surveys by the Scottish Survey of Assessment (SSA) (SEED, 2005c) and the Assessment of Performance Unit (APU) when this existed in England, Wales and Northern Ireland (DES/WO/DENI, 1989).

Reliability

The reliability of the assessment of performance in a subject domain depends on the reliability of individual items and on the number that are included. Using only a small number of items, designed to test individual students, restricts the range of performance that is assessed, and merely collecting the same data from a larger number of students at the national level will not increase the reliability of the assessment of the subject domain. Less reliably assessed but important aspects of achievement, such as the application of knowledge and skills, can be included and contribute to a more reliable measure by increasing the number of items, spread across different contexts. In surveys, optimum design calls for a balance between adequate sampling of the student population and adequate sampling of the subject domain: in this perspective, blanket uniform national tests are far from optimum, being over-sampled on the population and under-sampled on the subject domain.

Impact

Surveys of the kind just described involve only a small proportion of schools on any one occasion and the results are not meaningful at the school level. Consequently they cannot be used to judge individual teachers and schools and so do not acquire 'high stakes'. Since teachers do not know which students will be given which items or tasks, the tests provide information about students' achievement that is not distorted by training and practising what is to be assessed. This is in contrast to the use of national test results for national monitoring in England, which the review by Tymms (2004) mentioned earlier showed to be useless for reporting changes in national standards. Any preparation for the tests in a sample survey approach would have to address the whole domain and so, in theory, depending on the description of the domain and the test items, this could have a positive impact on students' experiences.

There is evidence that, in the APU and in on-going surveys such as the New Zealand National Education Monitoring Project (NEMP, 2006) and the SSA, both the description of the domains and their illustration in the test items are useful to policy makers and practitioners. This positive impact arises in part because the test constructs are not bound by the constraints of blanket testing. By contrast, taking information gathered by testing every individual student, and using these results to set national or local targets, forces attention on to the narrow range of outcomes assessed by these tests, bringing with it the negative impacts on students' learning experiences that have been identified earlier.

Resources

The economical advantage of collecting achievement data already available, as in using national tests for identifying national trends, must be judged against the extent to which it provides useful and relevant information. Similarly, the more costly process of establishing and running surveys covering a wide range of educational outcomes has to be judged against providing more detailed feedback that can be useful at the policy level, but also directly to practitioners. Separating monitoring from the performance of individual students would obviate the need for central collection of student assessment data. In turn, this would set student summative assessment free from the high stakes that restrict what is taught to what is assessed, whether by tests or teachers' assessment.

Consequences of Change

The complexity of an assessment system means that making change in how summative assessment is carried out involves a good deal more than replacing tests with teachers' judgments. This section looks at what may need to be changed in the curriculum, pedagogy and other parts of the assessment system if we are to ensure that summative assessment by teachers can match the requirements of validity, reliability, impact and resources.

Interaction with the Curriculum

The argument that teachers' assessment can provide highly valid information because it can use evidence from all learning activities holds only as long as those learning activities do in fact cover the full breadth of the intended curriculum. The potential for the assessment of deep rather than shallow learning, of learning how to learn and of the range of outcomes that users want to have included, as reported in Chapter 3, can only be realized if the content and pedagogy support their development.

Where tests have dominated assessment and virtually determined the curriculum, a change to the full implementation of a wider range of learning goals is bound to take time. In many situations, the concepts of learning with understanding, of understanding how to learn, of a learner-centred pedagogy, of using students' ideas, and so on, remain no more than slogans. The rhetoric concerning them can be ignored because they are not assessed. As this situation changes, there is a need for clarity about what these things mean in operation and which experiences will help students with these areas of learning.

Students will notice a difference in the curriculum they experience and parents will find a change in the information they receive about progress. At first there may be a negative reaction to the absence of familiar test and examination scores and their replacement by levels and comments relating to criteria. As we saw in Chapter 3, some students and parents like tests and they will need to be reassured that change will enhance learning – through enabling assessment to be used to help learning and providing more meaningful summative reports.

Refining Summative Assessment Criteria

Identifying criteria at the optimum level of detail for summative assessment is one of the steps that may need to be taken to support the reliability of teachers' judgments. It will not obviate the need for moderation but will make it easier. Finding just what is the optimum amount of detail is, of course, important and may need some discussion and investigation. The research mentioned in Chapter 5 and the examples of practices in Chapters 6 and 7 provide some clues.

Very detailed criteria that closely identify the evidence needed would be too numerous to be manageable. In any case, the experience of the NVQ assessment shows the danger of highly specific indicators, which can be 'ticked off' in a mechanistic way, losing sight of the whole through looking only at the constituent parts. Learning becomes fragmented. Moreover, it is difficult to see how conceptual understanding, cognitive skills and attitudes could be reduced to a series of simple outcomes. At the other end of the scale of detail, however, general statements such as 'understanding scientific enquiry' give too little idea of what evidence is needed and how it would be judged.

We can get some help in judging the most useful point between these extremes from the successful operation of assessment by teachers in Queensland. Among the essential characteristics of the Senior Certificate assessment procedures are some significant points about the way teachers make judgments of students' performance. These judgments are made against performance standards, which indicate both the dimensions of performance that are to be considered and the levels of the quality of performance within each one (Maxwell, 2004). As briefly indicated in Chapter 7, the evidence is accumulated in a portfolio, whose contents change over time as earlier pieces are replaced by later ones showing better performance. The end result is a judgment of how the final collection of evidence compares with the criteria of the graded categories used for reporting.

The particular number of reporting levels used in the Senior Certificate is less relevant than the overall approach. As Maxwell points out, 'for this approach to work, it is necessary to express the learning expectations in terms of common dimensions of learning (criteria)' (Maxwell, 2004: 3). The examples of criteria used in the Senior Certificate show that these are spelled out in rather more detail than, for example, the level descriptions in the English National Curriculum, but are still general enough to apply to a range of specific content. Thus providing level descriptions (standards), in the detail that experience seems to show is needed to support teachers' judgments, may require more than the reorganization of existing material. It requires the identification of *progression* in learning, based on what is known from research about the development of ideas and skills in particular domains of learning.

Use of Tests or Tasks

There are several ways in which special tasks or tests are used within a system of summative assessment that is essentially intended to be teacher-based. They fall into two groups: some where the special tasks for students provide some, or all, of the evidence teachers use for making judgments; others where they are used in moderating teachers' judgments based on evidence from regular work. Both have been mentioned in earlier chapters. Here we bring together some points about the pros and cons of these uses.

In relation to the first group, where tasks are used for evidence of performance, there appears to be a considerable difference between primary and secondary school experience. For both, the arguments in favour of using special tasks relate to providing well-designed tasks that are designed to enable students to show, and teachers to judge, particular performance. They have value in providing operational definitions of certain learning goals, which is of special value to inexperienced teachers. They can also 'plug gaps' where regular activities have, for one reason or another, not provided opportunities for teachers to judge students' performance.

Even though such tasks and tests are optional, the experience in primary schools within the context of helping with teachers' assessment is that tasks are regarded as providing the best evidence. Through the special attention their use receives, they acquire many of the disadvantages of tests. It may be that this is a consequence of the prevailing 'testing' culture and that teachers will only develop the confidence to use their own judgments of regular work if they have no alternative. However, if the tasks are designed to enrich students' experience and exemplify how higher level cognitive skills can be assessed their use can be of support in making best use of teachers' assessment.

In secondary schools, where subject teachers have much less opportunity for frequent observation of individual students than do class teachers in primary schools, there is a greater need for special tasks that extend the range of activities to cover all parts of the curriculum. Tasks that are developed by groups of teachers to cover aspects that they find difficult to assess in the normal course of work – such as engaging in a mathematical investigation, for example – are of particular value. The combined thinking that goes into them saves time for individual teachers in developing such activities for themselves. Some 'top-down' approaches to providing tasks are likely to be less effective in meeting teachers' needs.

There is no sharp distinction between the two uses of tasks and tests – for help in making judgments and for moderating judgments – when they are readily available to teachers or when they are required to use tests as well. For example, at the end of Key Stage tests in England, the teachers' judgments and test results in the core subjects are reported alongside each other and are said to have equal weight. The rationale for reporting both is that they are intended to assess different types of performance. But evidence from QCA surveys shows that many teachers include the test results in the evidence they use to form their judgments and so the value of using separate sources of evidence is compromised. In any case, teachers know that it is only the test results that matter, since these are used for setting targets and evaluating schools' performance.

In the Scottish system, too, the role of tests is ambiguous. Teachers are advised to use national tests when they judge from their classroom evidence that a student (or group of students) has reached a certain level of performance. The intention, then, is overtly for the test to function as moderation of teachers' judgments. But if the results do not agree – since they are based on different evidence they may well differ – then teachers will use the test results as evidence in reconsidering their judgments. However, teachers do not have to use tests and can moderate their judgments in other ways, such as through group consensus meetings. Without the high stakes attached to the results in Scotland, there is much less imperative to use tests.

The Need for Transparent Assessment

A good deal of the emotion that is aroused by assessment, particularly summative assessment, results from a fear or suspicion of the unknown. Students and teachers know full well that there is a lottery in the selection of questions for any test, since it cannot encompass all parts of what has been studied. Although the steps taken to ensure fairness in tests and examinations are quite elaborate (certainly costly) they take place within the unavoidable constraints of a test or examination system. In the light of these constraints and the disadvantages of tests pointed out in this book, it is the decision to use them that is less easy to explain. But while it may be fairer for teachers to assess students on what they have done in all their work, it is the process of judgment that attracts suspicion.

To take the fear and suspicion away from summative assessment we need to be completely open about the need for and purpose of assessment and why it is carried out in particular ways. Those more closely involved ought to be fully aware of how evidence is gathered and how judgments are made. Even the youngest students can be given some explanation of what evidence they and their teachers can use to judge whether they are making progress. The more open we are about assessment procedures the easier it is for students to assess their own work. This is vital for using assessment to help learning, but equally important for summative assessment so that there are no surprises (for students or parents) in reports of the level reached at a particular time. When students and parents expect teachers to be the only ones to say how students are doing, it will take time to establish a different and more collaborative relationship.

Demystifying summative assessment is an important measure to take in reducing negative impact. A further step, as suggested earlier (see p. 141) would be to remove the high stakes due to using results for school evaluation. Without this particular importance attached to results at the end of a Key Stage, there would be no reason to give special attention to assessment in these years, thus relieving teachers of these years from the burden of assessment they currently feel.

A Different Use of Time

A concern raised often by teachers about greater use of their judgments for summative assessment is that it will take too much time. This worry can arise from considering assessment and teaching to be separate activities, so that giving teachers a greater role in assessment is assumed to mean more time spent on that part of their work thus increasing the overall time. A change in how assessment is practised in the way argued here, however, means that it is more integrated with teaching, particularly when formative and summative purposes are brought together as discussed in Chapter 8. Teachers will be using evidence they gather during learning activities; they do not need to stop teaching to create tests or use school resources in purchasing tests in order to find out how their students are performing. If the evidence is gradually accumulated, in collaboration with students in a formative process, only the latest and best need to be judged against level descriptions at the time of reporting. Further, as noted on several occasions, moderating these final judgments has an important professional development function.

Moderation procedures require teachers to have time out of class, which can be a considerable obstacle to implementing the changes proposed. However, there are many ways of arranging for more out-of-class time so that teachers can meet within their school and with others from different schools in a district. The possibilities include reserving two or three days a term, or regular half-days each week, for professional development when students are not in school. Learning time is saved by spending less on tests (see Chapter 4) but can also be made up by adjusting school hours on other days. Overall, time may not be reduced but it will be used in far more professionally satisfying ways than in drilling students to pass tests.

There are also good reasons, beyond the efficient use of time, to make sure that summative assessment is an infrequent event, or certainly no more frequent than is really necessary. For internal summative assessment this is generally once or twice a year and for external uses only when required for major decisions. More frequent external testing, as currently experienced by students in England (who may be given either statutory or optional external tests in several subjects in every year throughout their school career (James, 2000)), inevitably results in a 'performance-oriented culture' (Pollard and Triggs, 2000) where there is little room for using assessment formatively. This culture is responsible for schools voluntarily exceeding what is required in terms of external assessment and judgments about levels reached by students.

Implications

All of these points have implications for those involved in framing policy at national and local levels, and for those who implement assessment policy in schools and colleges, for advisors and inspectors and for teacher educators. Whilst teachers and schools are dependent on policy decisions, it is also the case that policy changes require understanding and appropriate action by those who must operate them in practice, particularly, as here, where trust and responsibility are involved. We begin at the policy level since in most systems this is where change needs to be made first. The points draw on those identified in the ARG booklet based on the ASF project findings (ARG, 2006).

National and local policy makers

Those responsible for policy should

- be helped to recognize that the financial and time burdens at national and school levels of current summative assessment policies based on testing are not justified by the value of the information gained;
- take steps to replace national testing, where it exists, by a requirement for reporting moderated teachers' judgments of pupil performance, and divert some of the time and money saved into quality assurance that enhances teaching and learning;
- review the role of teacher assessment in examinations for 16 and 18 year olds;
- promote open discussion of why and how changes in the system are being made and how new procedures will operate;
- set up expert groups to develop criteria that indicate progression in development in a form appropriate to use in summative assessment of levels of achievement;
- replace the use of tests and examination results as the measure of school effectiveness by a range of indicators for use by inspectors and for school self-evaluation;
- replace the use of national test results for monitoring national standards by a system of sampling pupils' performance for national monitoring, thereby reducing the overall test burden whilst increasing the breadth and validity of the evidence.

Inspectors and advisors

Inspectors and local authority advisors should

- help schools to review school policies and practices to ensure that assessment is being used formatively and that this use is not overshadowed by summative tests and tasks;
- provide support for teachers in gathering and using a range of evidence from regular activities to report students' achievements;
- ensure that continuing professional development in assessment is available for those who require it;
- review the thoroughness of moderation and other procedures for quality assurance of summative assessment and the extent to which these procedures benefit teaching and learning;
- help schools to develop action plans based on self-evaluation across a range of measures rather than only on levels achieved by pupils.

School management

Those with management roles and responsibilities in schools should

- establish a school policy for assessment that supports assessment for learning at all times and requires summative assessment only when necessary for checking and reporting progress;
- provide protected time for quality assurance of all summative assessment, including any tests given by teachers, so that decisions made within a school about the progress of students are based on dependable information;
- ensure that parents understand how assessment is helping learning and how criteria are used in reporting progress;
- resist pressure for 'hard' data from tests and encourage the use of a range of types of evidence of students' learning.

Teachers

Teachers and teaching assistants should

- ensure that assessment is always used to help learning and that, when a summative assessment report is needed, the best evidence is reliably judged against relevant criteria;
- involve students in self-assessment of all their work in relation to lesson goals;
- help students to understand the criteria used in assessing their work for reporting purposes and how summative judgments are made;
- take part in moderation of summative judgments and other quality assurance procedures;
- use tests only when most appropriate, not as routine.

Teacher educators

Those involved in initial teacher education and professional development course providers should

- ensure that courses allow adequate time for
  - discussion of the different purposes of assessment and the uses made of assessment data;
  - trainee and serving teachers to identify, sample and evaluate different ways of gathering evidence of students' performance;
  - giving experience of generating assessment criteria linked to specific learning goals;
  - considering evidence of bias and other sources of error in assessment and how they can be minimized.

References

Adams, R. and Wilson, M. (1996) Formulating the Rasch model as a mixed coefficients multinomial logit, in G. Englehard and M. Wilson (eds), *Objective Measurement III: Theory into practice*. Norwood, NJ: Ablex.

ACCAC (Qualifications, Curriculum and Assessment Authority for Wales) (2004) *Review of the School Curriculum and Assessment Arrangements 5–16*. Cardiff: ACCAC.

ARG (Assessment Reform Group) (2006) *The Role of Teachers in the Assessment of Learning*. Obtainable from the ARG website: www.assessment-reform-group.org and from the CPA office of the Institute of Education, University of London.

ARG (Assessment Reform Group) (2004) *Testing, Motivation and Learning*. Obtainable from the ARG website: www.assessment-reform-group.org and from the CPA office of the Institute of Education, University of London.

ARG (Assessment Reform Group) (2002a) *Testing, Motivation and Learning*. Obtainable from the ARG website: www.assessment-reform-group.org and from the CPA office of the Institute of Education, University of London.

ARG (Assessment Reform Group) (2002b) *Assessment for Learning: 10 Principles*. Obtainable from the ARG website: www.assessment-reform-group.org and from the CPA office of the Institute of Education, University of London.

ASCL (Association for School and College Leaders) (2006) *Chartered Examiners*. Policy Paper 13. Leicester: ASCL.

Baker, E.L. and O'Neil, H.F. (1994) Performance Assessment and Equity: a view from the USA, *Assessment in Education*, 1: 11–26.

Bennett, R.E., Gottesman, R.L., Rock, D.A. and Cerullo, F. (1993) Influence of behaviour perceptions and gender on teachers' judgments of students' academic skill, *Journal of Educational Psychology*, 85: 347–56.

Bergan, J.R., Sladeczek, I.E., Schwarz, R.D. and Smith, A.N. (1991) Effects of a measurement and planning system on kindergarteners' cognitive development and educational programming, *American Educational Research Journal*, 28: 683–714.

Black, P. (2004) 'Issues in assessment'. Paper presented at the Assessment Systems for the Future project seminar, January 2004, available on the ARG website www.assessment-reform-group.org.

Black, P. (1998) *Testing: Friend or Foe? Theory and Practice of Assessment and Testing*. London: Falmer.

Black, P. (1993) Formative and summative assessment by teachers, *Studies in Science Education*, 21: 49–97.

Black, P. and Wiliam, D. (2006) The reliability of assessment, in J. Gardner (ed.), *Assessment and Learning*. London: Sage.

Black, P. and Wiliam, D. (1998a) Assessment and Classroom Learning, *Assessment in Education*, 5: 1–74.

Black, P. and Wiliam, D. (1998b) *Inside the Black Box*. Slough: NFER-Nelson.

Black, P., Harrison, C., Lee, C., Marshall, B. and Wiliam, D. (2003) *Assessment for Learning: Putting it into practice*. Maidenhead: Open University Press.

Black, P., Harrison, C., Lee, C., Marshall, B. and Wiliam, D. (2002) *Working Inside the Black Box*. Slough: NFER-Nelson.

Black, P., Harrison, C., Osborne, J. and Duschl, R. (2004) *Assessment of Science 14–19*. Published on the Royal Society website: www.royalsoc.ac.uk/education.

Black, P., McCormick, R., James, M. and Pedder, D. (2006a) Learning how to learn and assessment for learning: a theoretical inquiry, *Research Papers in Education*, 21 (2): 119–32.

Black, P., Swann, J. and Wiliam, D. (2006b) School pupils' beliefs about learning, *Research Papers in Education*, 21 (2): 151–70.

Boyle, B. and Bragg, J. (2006) A curriculum without foundation, *British Educational Research Journal*, 32 (4): 569–82.

Bransford, J.D., Brown, A.L. and Cocking, R.R. (eds) (1999) *How People Learn: Brain, mind, experience and school*. Washington, DC: National Academy Press.

Brookhart, S. and DeVoge, J. (1999) Testing a theory about the role of classroom assessment in pupil motivation and achievement, *Applied Measurement in Education*, 12: 409–25.

Brown, C.R. (1998) An evaluation of two different methods of assessing independent investigations in an operational pre-university level examination in biology in England, *Studies in Educational Evaluation*, 24: 78–96.

Bullock, K., Bishop, K.N., Martin, S. and Reid, A. (2002) Learning from coursework in English and geography, *Cambridge Journal of Education*, 32: 325–40.

Butler, R. (1988) Enhancing and undermining intrinsic motivation: the effects of task-involving and ego-involving evaluation on interest and performance, *British Journal of Education Psychology*, 58: 1–14.

Crooks, T.J. (1988) The impact of classroom evaluation practices on students, *Review of Educational Research*, 58: 438–81.

Cumming, J.J. and Maxwell, G.S. (2004) Assessment in Australian schools: current practice and trends, *Assessment in Education*, 11 (1): 89–108.

Daugherty, R. and Ecclestone, K. (2006) Constructing assessment for learning in the UK policy environment, in J. Gardner (ed.), *Assessment and Learning*. London: Sage.

Davidson, J. (2006) 'Education Policy in a Devolved Wales'. Address to the 3rd International Summit Conference for Leadership in Education, held Boston, November 2–4.

Deakin Crick, R., Broadfoot, P. and Claxton, G. (2002) *Developing ELLI: the Effective Lifelong Learning Inventory in Practice*. Bristol: Graduate School of Education, University of Bristol.

DES/WO (1988) *Task Group on Assessment and Testing: A report*. London: Department of Education and Science and Welsh Office.

DES/WO/DENI (1989) *National Assessment: the APU Science Approach*. London: HMSO.

DfES (2007) *Making Good Progress*. Consultation. London: Department for Education and Skills.

DfES Citizenship website at http://www.dfes.gov.uk/citizenship/, accessed 2006.

DfES and OfSTED (2004) *A New Relationship with Schools: Improving performance through school self-evaluation*. London: Department for Education and Skills and Office for Standards in Education.

Donnelly, J.F., Buchan, A.S., Jenkins, E.W. and Welford, A.G. (1993) *Policy, Practice and Teachers' Professional Judgment: The internal assessment of practical work in GCSE Science*. Driffield: Nafferton.

DTI and DfEE (2001) *Opportunity for All in a World of Change*. London: DTI and DfEE.

Dweck, C.S. (2000) *Self-Theories: Their role in motivation, personality and development*. Philadelphia, PA: Psychology Press.

Estyn (2004a) *Guidance on the Inspection of Primary and Nursery Schools*. Cardiff: Estyn.

Estyn (2004b) *Guidance on the Inspection of Secondary Schools*. Cardiff: Estyn.

Flexer, R.J., Cumbo, K., Borko, H., Mayfield, V. and Marion, S.F. (1995) How 'messing about' with performance assessment in mathematics affects what happens in classroom. Technical Report 396. Center for Research on Evaluation, Standards and Student Testing (CRESST): Los Angeles. Available from website http//cresst96.cse.ucla.edu/reports/tech396.pdf.

Frederiksen, J. and White, B. (2004) Designing assessment for instruction and accountability: an application of validity theory to assessing scientific inquiry, in M. Wilson (ed.), *Towards Coherence between Classroom Assessment and Accountability, 103rd Yearbook of the National Society for the Study of Education Part II.* Chicago, IL: National Society for the Study of Education. pp. 74–104.

Fuchs, L.S. and Fuchs, D. (1986) Effects of systematic formative evaluation: a meta-analysis, *Exceptional Children,* 53: 199–208.

Gardner, J. and Cowan, P. (2005) The fallibility of high stakes '11 plus' testing in Northern Ireland, *Assessment in Education,* 12 (2): 145–65.

Gipps, C. (1994) *Beyond Testing.* London: Falmer.

Gipps, C. and Clarke, S. (1998) *Monitoring the Consistency in Teacher Assessment and the Impacts of SCAA's Guidance Materials at Key Stages 1, 2 and 3.* London: Qualifications and Curriculum Authority.

Gipps, C., McCallum, B. and Brown, M. (1996) Models of teacher assessment among primary school teachers in England, *The Curriculum Journal,* 7: 167–83.

Good, F.J. (1988) Differences in marks awarded as a result of moderation: some findings from a teachers assessed oral examination in French, *Educational Review,* 40: 319–31.

Greene, T. (2006) 'There's more to education than exams', *The Independent,* Thursday 17 August: 35.

Griffin, P.E. (1989) *Developing Literacy Profiles.* Coburg, Victoria: Assessment Research Centre, Phillip Institute of Technology.

Hall, K. and Harding, A. (2002) Level descriptions and teacher assessment in England: towards a community of assessment practice, *Educational Research,* 44: 1–15.

Hall, K., Webber, B., Varley, S., Young, V. and Dorman, P. (1997) A study of teachers' assessment at Key Stage 1, *Cambridge Journal of Education,* 27: 107–22.

Hargreaves, D.H. (2003) *Education Epidemic.* London: Demos.

Hargreaves, D.J., Galton, M.J. and Robinson, S. (1996) Teachers' assessments of primary children's classroom work in the creative arts, *Educational Research,* 38: 199–211.

Hargreaves, E. (2007) The validity of collaborative assessment for learning, *Assessment in Education.*

Harland, J., Moor, H., Kinder, K. and Ashworth, M. (2003) *Talking 4: The Pupil Voice on the Key Stage 4 Curriculum: Report 4 of the Northern Ireland Curriculum Cohort Study.* Belfast: CCEA.

Harland, J., Moor, H., Kinder, K. and Ashworth, M. (2001) *Is the Curriculum Working? The Key Stage 3 Phase of the Northern Ireland Curriculum Cohort Study.* Slough: NFER.

Harland, J., Ashworth, M., Bower, R., Hogarth, S., Montgomery, A. and Moor, H. (1999a) *Real Curriculum at the start of Key Stage 3: Report Two from the Northern Ireland Curriculum Cohort Study*. Slough: NFER.

Harland, J., Kinder, K., Ashworth, M., Montgomery, A., Moor, H. and Wilkin, A. (1999b) *Real Curriculum: At the End of Key Stage 2: Report One from Northern Ireland*. Slough: NFER.

Harlen, W. (2006a) *Teaching, Learning and Assessing Science 5–12*. (4th edition). London: Sage.

Harlen, W. (2006b) On the relationship between assessment for formative and summative purposes, in J. Gardner (ed.), *Assessment and Learning*. London: Sage.

Harlen, W. (2006c) The role of assessment in developing motivation for learning, in J. Gardner (ed.), *Assessment and Learning*. London: Sage.

Harlen, W. (2004*) A systematic review of the reliability and validity of assessment by teachers used for summative purposes, in* Research Evidence in Education Library, Issue 1. London: EPPI-Centre, Social Sciences Research Unit, Institute of Education.

Harlen, W. (1994) Towards quality in assessment, in W. Harlen (ed.), *Enhancing Quality in Assessment*. London: Paul Chapman.

Harlen, W. and Deakin Crick, R. (2003) Testing and motivation for learning, *Assessment in Education*, 10 (2): 169–208.

Hautamäki, J., Kupiainen, S., Arinen, P., Hautamäki, A., Niemivirta, M., Rantanen, P., Ruuth, M. and Scheinin, P. (2005) Oppimaan oppiminen ala-asteella 2. Tilanne vuonna 2003 ja muutokset vuodesta 1996. (Learning-to-learn at the end of primary school, Results 2003 and changes from 1996). Oppimistulosten arviointi 2. Helsinki: Opetushallitus.

Hutchinson, C. and Hayward, L. (2005) The journey so far: assessment for learning in Scotland, *The Curriculum Journal*, 16 (2): 225–48.

Hutchinson, C. and Pirie, M. (2005) 'Views of Scottish parents about what matters in learning and assessment'. Paper presented at the ASF Seminar, July. (available at http://k1.ioe.ac.uk/tlrp/arg/ASF%20Report%205%20Appendix%20D.pdf).

IEA (Institute of Educational Assessors) (2006) Website available at www.ioea.org.uk.

Iredale, C. (1990) Pupils' attitudes towards GASP (Graded Assessment in Science Project), *School Science Review*, 72: 133–37.

James, M. (2000) Measured lives: the rise of assessment as the engine of change in English schools, *The Curriculum Journal*, 11 (3): 343–64.

James, M. and Pedder, D. (2006) Beyond method: assessment and learning practices and values, *The Curriculum Journal*, 17 (2): 109–38.

James, M., Black, P., McCormick, R., Pedder, D. and Wiliam, D. (2006) Learning how to learn in classrooms, schools and networks: aims, design and analysis, *Research Papers in Education*, 21 (2): 101–18.

Johnston, J. and McClune, W. (2000) Selection project sel 5.1: Pupil motivation and attitudes – self-esteem, locus of control, learning disposition and the impact of selection on teaching and learning, in *The Effects of the Selective System of Secondary Education in Northern Ireland*: Research Papers, Volume II. Bangor, Co Down: Department of Education. pp. 1–37.

Koretz, D., Stecher, B.M., Klein, S.P. and McCaffrey, D. (1994) The Vermont Portfolio Assessment Program: findings and implications, *Educational Measurement: Issues & Practice*, 13: 5–16.

Kulik, C-L.C. and Kulik, J.A. (1987) Mastery testing and student learning: a meta-analysis, *Journal of Educational Technology Systems*, 15: 325–45.

Leonard, M. and Davey, C. (2001) *Thoughts on the 11 plus*. Belfast: Save the Children Fund.

Linn, R.L. (2000) Assessments and Accountability, *Educational Researcher*, 29 (2): 4–16.

Marshall, B. and Drummond, M.J. (2006) How teachers engage with Assessment for Learning: lessons from the classroom, *Research Papers in Education*, 21 (2): 133–50.

Masters, G. and Forster, M. (1996) *Progress Maps*. Camberwell, Victoria, Australia: ACER.

Maxwell, G.S. (2004) 'Progressive assessment for learning and certification: some lessons from school-based assessment in Queensland'. Paper presented at the third conference of the Association of Commonwealth Examination and Assessment Boards, redefining the roles of educational assessment, March, Nadi, Fiji.

McIntyre, D., Pedder, D. and Rudduck, J. (2005) Pupil voice: comfortable and uncomfortable learnings for teachers, *Research Papers in Education*, 20 (2): 149–68.

Messick, S. (1989) Validity, in R.L. Linn (ed.), *Educational Measurement* (3rd edition). London: Collier Macmillan. pp. 12–103.

Millar, R. and Osborne, J. (eds) (1998) *Beyond 2000: Science Education for the Future*. Available on the King's College website at www.kcl.ac.uk/education and from King's College London, School of Education.

Millar, R., Leach, J., Osborne, J. and Ratcliffe, M. (eds) (2006) *Improving Subject Teaching. Lessons from research in science education*. London: Routledge.

Natriello, G. (1987) The impact of evaluation processes on students, *Educational Psychologist*, 22: 155–75.

NEMP (National Education Monitoring Project) (2006) See website at http://nemp.otago.ac.nz/index.htm.

OECD (Organisation for Economic Co-operation and Development) (2000) *Measuring Student Knowledge and Skills*. Paris: OECD.

OECD (Organisation for Economic Co-operation and Development) (1999) *Measuring Student Knowledge and Skills: A New Framework for Assessment*. Paris: OECD.

Paechter, C. (1995) 'Doing the Best for the Students': dilemmas and decisions in carrying out statutory assessment tasks, *Assessment in Education*, 2: 39–52.

Pilcher, J.K. (1994) The value-driven meaning of grades, *Educational Assessment*, 2: 69–88.

Pine, J., Aschbacher, P., Rother, E., Jones, M., McPhee, C., Martin, C., Phelps, S., Kyle, T. and Foley, B. (2006) Fifth graders' science inquiry abilities: a comparative study of students in hands-on and textbook curricula, *Journal of Research in Science Teaching*, 43 (5): 467–84.

Pollard, A. and Triggs, P. (2000) *Policy, Practice and Pupil Experience*. London: Continuum International.

Pollard, A., Triggs, P., Broadfoot, P., McNess, E. and Osborn, M. (2000) *What Pupils Say: Changing policy and practice in primary education*. London: Continuum.

QCA (Qualifications and Curriculum Authority) (2006a) *Monitoring Pupils' Progress in English at KS3* (Final report on the 2003–5 pilot). London: QCA.

QCA (Qualifications and Curriculum Authority) (2006b) *Teachers' Views on Coursework Research conducted by Ipsos Mori for QCA*. London: QCA.

QCA (Qualifications and Curriculum Authority) (2006c) *A Review of GCSE Coursework*. London: QCA.

QCA (Qualifications and Curriculum Authority) (2005) *A Review of GCE and GCSE Coursework Arrangements*. London: QCA.

QCA (Qualifications and Curriculum Authority) (2004) 'Financial Modelling of the English Examinations System, 2003–4'. Report from PriceWaterhouseCoopers (PWC) for the QCA. Available at http://www.qca.org.uk/12130.html.

QCA (Qualifications and Curriculum Authority) (2003) *Foundation Stage Profile Handbook*. London: QCA.

Radnor, H.A. (1996) *Evaluation of Key Stage 3 Assessment Arrangements for 1995: Final Report*. Exeter: University of Exeter.

Reay, D. and Wiliam, D. (1999) 'I'll be a nothing': structure, agency and the construction of identity through assessment, *British Educational Research Journal*, 25: 343–45.

Reeves, D.J., Boyle, W.F. and Christie, T. (2001) The relationship between teacher assessment and pupil attainments in standard test/tasks at key stage 2, 1996–8, *British Educational Research Journal*, 27: 141–60.

Resnick, L.B. and Resnick, D.P. (1992) Assessing the thinking curriculum: new tools for educational reform, in B.G. Gifford and M.C. O'Connor (eds), *Changing Assessments: Alternative views of aptitude, achievements and instruction*. Boston: Kluwer. pp. 37–75.

Rowe, K.J. and Hill, P.W. (1996) Assessing, recording and reporting students' educational progress: the case for 'subject profiles', *Assessment in Education*, 3: 309–52.

Satterly, D. (1994) Quality in external assessment, in W. Harlen (ed.), *Enhancing Quality in Assessment*. London: Paul Chapman.

Schunk, D. (1996) Goal and self-evaluative influences during children's cognitive skill learning, *American Educational Research Journal*, 33: 359–82.

SEED (Scottish Executive Education Department) (2005a) *Assessment is for Learning* (Information sheet). Edinburgh: SEED.

SEED (Scottish Executive Education Department) (2005b) Circular 02, June. Edinburgh: SEED.

SEED (Scottish Executive Education Department) (2005c) *Information Sheet on the Scottish Survey of Achievement*. Edinburgh: SEED.

SEED (Scottish Executive Education Department) (2004) *Assessment, Testing and Reporting 3–14: Our response*. Edinburgh: SEED.

SEED (Scottish Executive Education Department) (2002) *How Good is Our School? Self evaluation using quality indicators*. Edinburgh: HMIE.

SHA (Secondary Heads Association, now the Association of School and College Leaders) (2004) Website available at http://www.ascl.org.uk/datafiles/hostFiles/host239/Policy%20paper%2013%20Chartered%20examiners%20FINAL%20priced.pdf.

Shapley, K.S. and Bush, M.J. (1999) Developing a valid and reliable portfolio assessment in the primary grades: building on practical experience, *Applied Measurement in Education*, 12: 11–32.

Sharpley, C.F. and Edgar, E. (1986) Teachers' ratings vs standardized tests: an empirical investigation of agreement between two indices of achievement, *Psychology in the Schools*, 23: 106–11.

Shavelson, R.J., Baxter, G.P. and Pine, J. (1992) Performance assessments: political rhetoric and measurement reality, *Educational Researcher*, 21, 22–7.

Sheffield Hallam University Centre for Science Education (2003) *The Cost of Assessment: A Report for the Royal Society*. Available from the Centre for Science Education, Sheffield Hallam University.

Smith, E. and Gorard, S. (2005) 'They don't give us our marks': the role of formative feedback in student progress, *Assessment in Education*, 12 (1): 21–38.

Tymms, P. (2004) Are standards rising in English primary schools?, *British Educational Research Journal*, 30 (4): 477–94.

Van der Linden, W. and Hambleton, R. (1996) *Handbook of Modern Item-Response Theory*. New York: Springer-Verlag.

Welford, G., Harlen, W. and Schofield, B. (1985) *Practical Testing at Ages 11, 13, and 15*. London: DES/WO/DENI.

White, R.T. (1988) *Learning Science*. Oxford: Blackwell.

White, B.Y. and Frederiksen, J.T. (1998) Inquiry, modeling and metacognition: making science accessible to all students, *Cognition and Instruction*, 16 (1): 3–118.

Wiliam, D. (2001) Reliability, validity and all that jazz, *Education 3–13*, 29 (3): 17–21.

Wilmut, J. (2004) 'Experiences of Summative Teacher Assessment in the UK'. A review conducted for the Qualifications and Curriculum Authority, unpublished.

Wilson, M. and Scalise, K. (2004) 'Using assessment to improve learning: The BEAR Assessment System'. Paper presented at the ASF project Seminar, March, in Cambridge, England. Available on the ARG website at www.assessment-reform-group.org/ASF.

Wiske, M.S. (ed.) (1998) *Teaching for Understanding*. San Francisco, CA: Jossey-Bass.

Author index

Subject index